JESUS *and the* JEWISH ROOTS
of MARY

JESUS *and the* JEWISH ROOTS *of* MARY

◇◇◇◇◇

Unveiling the Mother of the Messiah

BRANT PITRE

IMAGE

New York

Nihil Obstat: Reverend Joshua Rodrigue, STL, Censor Librorum
Imprimatur: Most Reverend Shelton J. Fabre, Bishop of Houma-Thibodaux

The *Nihil Obstat* and *Imprimatur* are official declarations that a book or
pamphlet is free of doctrinal or moral error. No implication is contained
therein that those who have granted the *Nihil Obstat* or *Imprimatur* agree
with the content, opinions, or statements expressed.

Library of Congress Cataloging-in-Publication Data
Names: Pitre, Brant James, author.
Title: Jesus and the Jewish roots of Mary : unveiling the Mother of
   the Messiah / Brant Pitre.
Description: New York : Crown Publishing Group, 2018.
Identifiers: LCCN 2018016355 (print) | LCCN 2018033742 (ebook) |
   ISBN 9780525572749 (e-book) | ISBN 9780525572732 (hardcover)
Subjects: LCSH: Mary, Blessed Virgin, Saint—Theology. | Mary,
   Blessed Virgin, Saint—History of doctrines. | Catholic Church—
   Relations—Judaism. | Judaism—Relations—Catholic Church.
Classification: LCC BT613 (ebook) | LCC BT613 .P58 2018 (print) |
   DDC 232.91—dc23
LC record available at https://lccn.loc.gov/2018016355

ISBN 978-0-525-57273-2
Ebook ISBN 978-0-525-57274-9

PRINTED IN THE UNITED STATES OF AMERICA

Book design: Andrea Lau
Jacket design: Sarah Horgan
Jacket photograph: Adoración de los Reyes *by Maestro de Perea,*
courtesy of Museo de Bellas Artes de Valencia

11th Printing

First Edition

For Aidan Nathanael,

My beloved son "in whom there is no guile."
(John 1:47)

Contents

◇◇◇◇◇

CONTENTS

"Behold, your mother!"

—JESUS OF NAZARETH (JOHN 19:27)

It is easier to depict the sun with its light and its heat,
Than to tell the story of Mary in its splendor . . .
Love moves me to speak of her.

—JACOB OF SERUG,
HOMILY 1 ON THE BLESSED VIRGIN[1]
(5TH–6TH CENTURY A.D.)

chapter 1

INTRODUCTION

◇◇◇◇◇

This book is written for anyone who has ever wondered what the Bible really teaches about Mary, the mother of Jesus. In particular, it is written for those who have been puzzled by, struggled with, or rejected Catholic beliefs about Mary as unbiblical—if not idolatrous. I should know. I was one of them. Here's how the story goes . . .

THE PROBLEM WITH MARY

When I was growing up, I had no problem believing what the Catholic Church teaches about Mary. I was born into a Catholic family, baptized as an infant, and raised in predominantly Catholic South Louisiana. Every Sunday, I attended a Catholic church that had several statues of Mary. On special occasions, I lit a candle and would ask Mary to pray for me. One of my earliest memories is of my mother taking my brothers and me to pray the Rosary with my grandmother and great-grandmother. While the women prayed, we boys would sit on the floor playing and listening and—if memory serves—getting pretty bored. However, by the time I was seven or eight years old, my older brother and I had picked up the practice for ourselves. Believe it or not, we boys used to kneel beside our beds at night for thirty to forty minutes while we read the Bible verses and said the prayers in a little book called *The Scriptural Rosary.*[1]

In the years that followed I would come to learn the basic teachings of the Catholic Church regarding Mary: that she was a virgin when she conceived Jesus (the virginal conception) and that she remained a virgin her whole life long (perpetual virginity). Eventually, I also learned that she was created without sin (immaculate conception) and remained sinless her whole life, and that, at the end of her life, she was taken up body and soul into heaven to be with the risen Jesus (bodily assumption). In all that time, it never once crossed my mind to question anything that the Church taught, believed, or practiced with regard to Jesus' mother. To me, Mary was a real person, an ordinary part of my life. When I read Mary's declaration that "all generations shall call me blessed" (Luke 1:48)—I knew that included me. Mary was the "Blessed Mother"—Jesus' mother and mine.

Things began to change, however, when I met my future wife, Elizabeth. Although she came from an even bigger Cajun family than mine—they had eight children, we had only six—she was not Catholic. Her family was Baptist. In fact, Elizabeth's late grandfather had been a very prominent Southern Baptist missionary, who founded many Baptist churches along the bayous of South Louisiana. Her grandmother was also a well-known and much-loved matriarch of the local Baptist churches, and an amazing Christian woman.[2] Given the predominantly Catholic population of South Louisiana, many of the members of her grandfather's churches were ex-Catholics who had left to become "Bible-believing Christians." In practice, this meant accepting the doctrine of the "Bible alone" (Latin *sola Scriptura*) and rejecting many Catholic doctrines and practices as contrary to Scripture. In particular, they were taught to reject the Catholic beliefs in Mary's perpetual virginity and sinlessness as unbiblical, and to regard practices such as praying the Rosary and venerating Mary—all widespread in the popular piety of Cajun Catholicism—as idolatry.

As you might expect, once Elizabeth and I began dating—at the ripe old age of fifteen—both she and her family began to ask questions about my beliefs. It was all the usual Protestant versus Catholic stuff: Why do you have statues in your churches when the Bible says make no "graven image"? Why do you baptize babies when they aren't old enough to personally accept Jesus as their Lord and Savior? Why can't Catholic priests get married? And so on. Given the fact that Elizabeth is both very smart and very pretty, and that I really wanted to remain her boyfriend, I did my best to learn about my faith and answer their questions sincerely. And for the most part, it seemed to work fine. Her mother and father continued to allow me to see her, and even though she and I still disagreed about key practices and beliefs, we respected one another and our different faiths. In our sophomore year in college, we decided to get married.

All that changed, dramatically, in the course of a single afternoon, not long before our wedding. Elizabeth and I had scheduled a meeting with the new pastor of her family's church in order to discuss getting married there. We assumed there would be no problems, since Elizabeth's grandfather had built the church himself. However, once we sat down in the pastor's office, what was supposed to be a brief meeting turned into a heated, two-hour-long interrogation of me by the pastor about my Catholic faith. Over and over again, he pommeled me with questions about purgatory, the saints, the pope, the Eucharist, and, of course, the Virgin Mary.

I wrote about this encounter in my earlier book *Jesus and the Jewish Roots of the Eucharist.*[3] There I told the story of how I went home that night particularly upset about the pastor's attack on the Catholic belief that the bread and wine of the Eucharist really become Jesus' body and blood. I also told how that night, while searching for answers, I opened my Bible to the passage where Jesus declares that his "flesh" and his "blood" are "real food" and "real drink" (John 6:53–58). In part, because I immediately stumbled onto this key biblical passage, I never really lost my faith in Jesus' real presence in the Eucharist.

However, the impact of the pastor's attack on my beliefs about *Mary* was different. When it came to Mary, I had no similar aha! moments. I did not go home and stumble onto passages in the Bible that clearly taught that she was immaculately conceived, that she had committed no sins, or that her body was assumed into heaven. To the contrary, from what I could tell, the New Testament had surprisingly little to say about Mary. Moreover, what it did say was sometimes cause for concern. In short, when it came to the biblical basis of my beliefs about Mary, the pastor had posed questions to which I had no answers. One question of his in particular stands out in my memory: the charge that Catholic veneration of Mary is not just unbiblical but *idolatrous*.

THE QUEEN OF HEAVEN?

"Why do you Catholics worship Mary?" the pastor fired off at me. "Don't you know God alone is to be worshiped?"

Having paid some attention in my catechism class, I was able to reply:

"As Catholics, we don't *worship* Mary. We *honor* her as the Mother of Jesus and the Queen of Heaven."

"'The Queen of Heaven'?" he retorted. "That's interesting. Do you know what the Bible says about the 'Queen of Heaven'?"

"No." I confessed. "What?"

Knowingly, he opened his Bible and after flipping a few pages, said: "It actually mentions the 'Queen of Heaven' in the book of Jeremiah. The Bible says she was a pagan goddess:

> [The LORD said to Jeremiah:] "Do you not see what they are doing in the cities of Judah and in the streets of Jerusalem? The children gather wood, the fathers kindle fire, *and the women knead dough, to make cakes for the queen of heaven;* and they pour out drink offerings *to other gods*, to provoke me to anger . . ." (Jeremiah 7:17–18).[4]

"There it is, right there!" he announced. "The worship of the 'Queen of Heaven'—exactly what you Catholics do to Mary—is condemned as idolatry."

I sat in stunned silence. Although I had put up a fight for many of my other beliefs, I had no idea how to respond to this. To say the least, none of my catechism classes had ever mentioned the "Queen of Heaven" in the book of Jeremiah. Nor had anyone ever explained to me how we could refer to Mary as the Queen of Heaven when the Bible used the same words for the name of a pagan goddess. I thought about my favorite prayer, the "Hail Holy Queen" (also known as the *Salve Regina*) which I had said countless times at the end of every Rosary. All I could think was *Is that what I've been doing my whole life? Committing idolatry without even knowing it?*

Knowing he had scored a serious point, the pastor moved on to another topic.

Fortunately, that meeting lasted only a couple of hours. However, the effect of the pastor's questions about Mary had a much longer impact on me. They were like a crack in the windshield of my childhood beliefs—one that started small and slowly spread till I could no longer see clearly. When I looked for the biblical foundations of other Catholic teachings, I found what I considered compelling evidence. However, when it came to Mary, I kept coming up short. I was at a loss. The more I read the few passages in the New Testament that even mention Mary, the more trouble I had finding anything like what the Catholic Church teaches. *Where is any of this in the Bible?* I wondered.

If you've studied the New Testament, you know what I mean. Where does it ever mention Mary's immaculate conception? Seemingly nowhere. To be sure, the angel Gabriel calls Mary "full of grace" (Luke 1:28)—at least in some translations—but that's not exactly the same thing as "immaculately conceived." Or how about the sinlessness of Mary? It seems to fly in the face of the apostle Paul's declaration that "all have sinned and fall short of the glory of God" (Romans 3:23). And what about Mary's bodily assumption into heaven? I couldn't seem to find that anywhere in the New Testament either. To be sure, the book of Revelation does describe a mysterious "woman" who is "in heaven" and is "clothed with the sun" (Revelation 12:1). However, I learned that many interpreters reject the idea that this "woman" is Mary (more on that later). In any case, neither Revelation nor any other book of the New Testament describes her being assumed into heaven. As for the perpetual virginity of Mary, it seems to be flatly contradicted by the New Testament, which explicitly mentions the "brothers" and "sisters" of Jesus (see Matthew 13:55; Mark 3:31–35, 6:3; 1 Corinthians 9:5).

Finally, to top it all off, whenever Mary does appear in the Gospels, instead of venerating her the way I had been taught to do, Jesus himself seems to disrespect her—or at least put her off in ways that, at least by today's standards, seem pretty rude. Think here of the wedding at Cana, where Jesus says to Mary: *"O woman, what have you to do with me? My hour has not yet come"* (John 2:4 RSV). What are we to make of this? (I can only imagine what my mother would do if I ever addressed her as "woman.") Why Jesus' seeming dismissal of Mary? It almost comes off like a preemptive strike against later devotion to her. How can Catholics say that we should honor Mary when Jesus himself seems to dishonor her?

The impact all of this had on my view of Mary was negative and long-lasting. While I continued to accept many Catholic teachings, my confidence in the doctrines and practices regarding Mary wavered, getting weaker and weaker. Not long after our wedding, I stopped praying the Rosary. Eventually, I began to harbor serious doubts about several of the Church's teachings about Mary—her immaculate conception, her bodily assumption, and her perpetual virginity. After all, Joseph and Mary were married, weren't they? Why shouldn't they have an ordinary marriage with other children? In the grand scheme of things, what difference did Mary's perpetual virginity actually make?

The years passed, and by the time I got to the University of Notre Dame, in 1999, to begin studying for my Ph.D. in theology, I had serious objections to many of the Catholic Church's official teachings about Mary. I also no longer practiced the Catholic devotions to Mary that were part of my childhood faith.

But then something dramatic happened, something that would alter the way I saw Mary forever, and would lay the foundations for the writing of this book. I began to discover the *Jewish roots* of Catholic beliefs about Mary.[5]

THROUGH ANCIENT JEWISH EYES

Most Ph.D. programs in biblical studies tend to specialize in either the New Testament or the Old Testament. At Notre Dame, however, the doctoral program was entitled Christianity and Judaism in Antiquity. This meant that all Ph.D.

students in biblical studies were required to take courses in both the New Testament and the Old Testament, both Greek and Hebrew, both early Christianity and ancient Judaism. It is hard for me to overemphasize how pivotal Notre Dame's both/and approach was in helping me to understand the Jewish roots of Catholic beliefs about Mary. In the course of my studies, I learned three things that completely changed the way I saw Mary.

First, I learned that Catholic beliefs about Mary are *deeply rooted in ancient Christianity*. As we will see over the course of this book, Mary's perpetual virginity, sinlessness, identity as "Mother of God," power of intercession, and bodily assumption into heaven are not new ideas but old—very old. Moreover, such beliefs were extremely widespread, held by Christians living in the Holy Land, Syria, Egypt, Greece, Asia Minor, Rome, and elsewhere. In short, they were part and parcel of the ancient Christian faith.[6]

Second, I gradually understood that these ancient Christian beliefs about Mary flowed directly out of what early Christians believed about Jesus. In the words of the *Catechism of the Catholic Church*:

> *What the Catholic faith believes about Mary is based on what it believes about Christ*, and what it teaches about Mary illumines in turn its faith in Christ. (CCC 487)[7]

I cannot overemphasize the significance of this principle. If you want to understand what the Bible teaches about Mary, you have to make sure you begin with what it teaches about Jesus. Therefore, in every chapter, before we look at Mary, we will consider Jesus.

Third, and most important of all, I discovered that *ancient Christians got their beliefs about Mary from the Old Testament*— not just the New Testament. In fact, the key to understanding what the Bible teaches about Mary can be found in what is called "typology": the study of Old Testament prefigurations (or "types") and their New Testament fulfillments. In the words of Joseph Ratzinger (who later became Pope Benedict XVI): "The image of Mary in the New Testament is woven entirely of Old Testament threads."[8] Along similar lines, the Protestant theologian Timothy George writes:

> Evangelicals have much to learn from reading Mary against the background of *Old Testament foreshadowings . . . The image of Mary in the New Testament is inseparable from its Old Testament antecedents*, without which we are left with not only a reductionist view of Mary, but also of Christ.[9]

This idea of looking at prefigurations of Mary in the Old Testament totally blew me away. I was familiar with looking at Jesus this way: for example, as the new Adam, the new Moses, the new Davidic king. But I had never even *heard* of studying the Bible's typology of Mary. For example, I never knew that the New Testament does depict Mary as a queen—but not the pagan "Queen of Heaven." Instead, it depicts her as the queen mother of the Messiah's kingdom. In ancient Israel, it was not the king's wife who was queen but his mother. The queen mother (Hebrew *gebirah*) was second only to the king himself. She was honored with a royal throne and functioned as the supreme royal intercessor with the king (2 Kings 1–2; Psalm 45).

Eventually, it dawned on me that the reason I had begun to consider Catholic beliefs about Mary "unbiblical" was that I was not paying enough attention to the Old Testament. And it wasn't just me. The more I read, the more I began to notice that virtually every book on Mary that rejected her sinlessness, perpetual virginity, bodily assumption, and other Catholic beliefs as unscriptural would invariably ignore the Old Testament.[10]

This is a big problem. You simply *cannot* understand Mary without looking at her in her first-century Jewish context. Scholars today agree that Jesus can be fully understood only from within the Judaism of his day. However, when it comes to Mary, the same rule does not seem to apply. Over and over again, books about Mary that are critical of Catholic beliefs completely ignore the Old Testament—to say nothing of ancient Jewish traditions outside the Bible. But if you are going to understand what the Bible really teaches about Mary, you can't just study the New Testament. It's not enough. You've got to go back to the Old Testament. You have to try to see both Jesus and Mary through ancient Jewish eyes.

That is what we are going to do in this book. We are going to go back and explore the *Jewish roots of Mary*. In order to do so, we will have to pay close attention to both Jewish Scripture and ancient Jewish tradition. Above all, the Old Testament will be the most important source for understanding what the New Testament says about Mary.

However, I will also quote from writings outside the Bible that reflect Jewish traditions from the time of Jesus and Mary: writings such as the Dead Sea Scrolls, the works of Josephus and Philo, the Jewish Pseudepigrapha, the ancient Aramaic Targums, and early literature of the rabbis. (For a full list of Jewish sources outside the Bible that we will be drawing on, see the Appendix.) Indeed, one of the unique aspects of this book is that we will study ancient Jewish traditions about the mother of the Messiah, traditions that never make it into most books on Jesus or Mary.

There's no doubt about it. When it comes to the mother of Jesus, the stakes are high. Mary is a dividing line between Christians. And the issues involved are serious. If Protestants are right about Mary, then both Catholic and Orthodox Christians—more than half of the world's Christian population—are committing idolatry on a regular basis. If Catholics and Orthodox are right about Mary, then Protestant Christians—a little less than half of the world's Christians—are missing out on what the Bible as a whole reveals about the mother of Christ.[11]

As I hope to show, far from being "unbiblical," Catholic doctrines about Mary are deeply rooted in Scripture—*if* you interpret the New Testament in the light of the Old Testament. Keep looking at the New Testament by itself, and you'll never see them. Start looking at Mary through ancient Jewish eyes, and all will become clear. Likewise, the Catholic practice of venerating Mary and asking for her prayers is deeply rooted in what the Bible reveals about who Mary is and what role she plays in the kingdom of God. Contrary to what some people believe, the Catholic Church did not get its teachings about Mary from paganism. It got them from *Judaism.*

So, whether you're a Christian who has always wondered what the Bible actually teaches about Mary; whether you're a Jew or a Muslim who is curious to learn more about the mother of Jesus; whether you're an agnostic or an atheist interested in the Jewish origins of Christianity—whatever your religious background or worldview—I invite you to come along with me on this journey and try to see the mother of Jesus through ancient Jewish eyes. I promise that, whoever you are, you are going to encounter new insights into the most influential woman in all of history. You might even discover why she is more than just the mother of Jesus, why ancient Christians called her the "mother of *all* the living" (cf. Genesis 3:22). Above all, I hope you'll find that the more deeply you understand Mary, the better you'll understand Jesus himself.

In order to see all this, however, we need to go back to the very beginning of the Jewish Bible, and to the first woman in the Old Testament. We need to begin with Eve.

chapter 2

THE NEW EVE

◇◇◇◇◇

As I said in Chapter 1, if you are going to understand who Mary is, you have to begin with Jesus. When it comes to the mission and message of Jesus, at the very center is "the Gospel": the "good news" (Greek *euangelion*) of salvation (Mark 1:14–15).

But what exactly is the "Gospel"? If you're anything like me, when I was a child I simply assumed that the "good news" was that Jesus the Savior had died for my sins so that I could go to heaven when I died. In other words, the bad news was that I was a sinner, but the good news was that Jesus offered me forgiveness. And to be sure, according to the New Testament, the forgiveness of sins is an essential part of Jesus' message. As he says to his disciples during the Last Supper: "This is my blood of the covenant, which is poured out for many for the forgiveness of sins" (Matthew 26:28).

However, the older I got, and the more I studied the New

Testament, the more I began to realize that the "good news" of salvation is about much more than just the forgiveness of my personal sins. It is about the forgiveness of the very first sin—the sin of Adam and Eve—through which suffering and death came into the world. According to the New Testament, Jesus is the new Adam, whose obedience undoes the disobedience of the first Adam.[1] Nowhere is this expressed more clearly than in the writings of the apostle Paul, who has this to say about Adam and Jesus:

> As one man's trespass led to condemnation for all men, so one man's act of righteousness leads to acquittal and life for all men. *For as by one man's disobedience many were made sinners, so by one man's obedience many will be made righteous.* (Romans 5:18–19)

> Thus it is written, *"The first man Adam* became a living being"; *the last Adam* became a life-giving spirit . . . The first man was from the earth, a man of dust; the second man is from heaven. (1 Corinthians 15:45, 47)

Once you begin to see Jesus as Paul saw him—as the "last Adam"—it changes the way you think about the "good news" of salvation. If Jesus is the new Adam, then salvation is not just about saving sinners from the fires of hell. It is about *undoing the effects of the Fall of Adam and Eve.* It is about restoring the original "righteousness" which Adam had when he was created but which he lost through disobedience

(Romans 5:17). It is about the power of God's "grace" to actually "make" human beings "righteous" (Romans 5:19).[2]

What does any of this have to do with Mary? The answer is simple: *If Jesus is the new Adam, then who is the new Eve?* According to the book of Genesis, Adam is not the only human being created by God and placed in the Garden of Eden. Moreover, Adam does not bring sin and death into the world alone. As Adam's partner, Eve plays an essential role in bringing about the fall of humankind.

In this chapter, we will begin our study of the Jewish roots of Mary by looking at how the New Testament depicts Mary as a new Eve. Once we begin to see Mary in this light, we will also begin to understand why ancient Christians did not believe she was just an ordinary woman. In particular, we will be able to understand why some of them believed that Mary, though fully human, was *sinless.* In order to see all this clearly, however, we have to go back to the beginning, and look a little more closely at the first Eve.

THE WOMAN IN EDEN

When it comes to the first woman in the Bible, an entire book could easily be written.[3] For our purposes here, I just want to make four key points about the figure of Eve in Jewish Scripture and ancient Jewish tradition.

Adam and Eve Are Created "Very Good"

First, according to the Jewish Bible, God creates the first man and the first woman in a state of moral goodness and immortality. Consider the two accounts of creation in the book of Genesis:

> So God created man in *his own image,* in the image of God he created him; *male and female he created them.* And God blessed them, and God said to them, "Be fruitful and multiply . . ." *And God saw everything that he had made, and behold, it was very good.* (Genesis 1:27–28, 31)

> The LORD God took the man and put him in *the garden of Eden* to till it and keep it. And the LORD God commanded the man, saying, *"You may freely eat of every tree of the garden;* but of the tree of the knowledge of good and evil you shall not eat, for in the day that you eat of it you shall die" . . . [Then] the LORD God caused a deep sleep to fall upon the man, and while he slept took one of his ribs and closed up its place with flesh; *and the rib which the LORD God had taken from the man he made into a woman* and brought her to the man. Then the man said, "This at last is bone of my bones and flesh of my flesh; *she shall be called Woman,* because she was taken out of Man." (Genesis 2:15–17, 21–23)

Notice here that not only are Adam and Eve created in God's "image" and "likeness"; they are also created "very good" (Hebrew *tōv meōd*) (Genesis 1:31). As one prominent Old Testament scholar points out, this Hebrew expression means that man and woman are created "just" or "morally good."[4]

In other words, they are created *without sin*. Notice also that they are given the gift of immortality. When God says that they may "freely eat" of any tree in the garden, this includes the fruit of the "tree of life," which—if they eat of it—they will "live forever" (Genesis 2:16, 9, 22).[5] Finally, it is worth noting that before the Fall, the woman is never actually called "Eve." She is simply called "woman." As Adam declares: "She shall be called Woman (Hebrew *'ishah*), because she was taken out of Man (Hebrew *'ish*)" (Genesis 2:23). If you keep reading Genesis, you will discover that Adam does not give her the name Eve until after they commit the first sin (Genesis 3:20).

Adam and Eve Fall Together

Second, according to the book of Genesis, Eve invites Adam to eat the forbidden fruit. This first sin is commonly referred to as "the Fall," even though the Bible itself does not use this language. While the story is very familiar, let's look at it again and pay close attention to what it does (and does not) say:

> Now *the serpent* was more subtle than any other wild creature that the LORD God had made. He said to *the woman*, "Did God say, 'You shall not eat of any tree of the garden'?" And the woman said to the serpent, "We may eat of the fruit of the trees of the garden; but God said, 'You shall not eat of the fruit of the tree which is in the midst of the garden, neither shall you touch it, lest you die.'" But the serpent said to the woman, "You will not die. For God knows that when you eat of it your eyes will

be opened, and you will be like God, knowing good
and evil." So when the woman saw that the tree
was good for food, and that it was a delight to the
eyes, and that the tree was to be desired to make
one wise, *she took of its fruit and ate; and she also gave
some to her husband, who was with her, and he ate.*
(Genesis 3:1–6)[6]

Contrary to what some artistic depictions suggest, Eve is
not alone when she commits the first sin. As Genesis makes
very clear, once Eve eats the fruit, she gives some to Adam,
"who was with her (Hebrew *'immah*)" (Genesis 3:6).[7] In other
words, Adam and Eve fall *together.* Eve cooperates with
Adam, and Adam cooperates with Eve. Neither acts in isola-
tion from the other.

This of course explains why both Adam and Eve suffer
the effects of the first sin. To the woman God says: "I will
greatly multiply your pain in childbearing; in pain you shall
bring forth children" (Genesis 3:16). To the man he says: "In
the sweat of your face you shall eat bread till you return to
the ground, for out of it you were taken; you are dust, and to
dust you shall return" (Genesis 3:19). This last line echoes
God's earlier warning about what will happen if the man
eats from the forbidden tree: "you shall surely die" (Genesis 2:16). Indeed, because of their actions, they are driven
out of the Garden of Eden; as a result, they are unable any
longer to eat of "the tree of life, and live forever" (Genesis
3:22). Through the first act of disobedience to God, Adam
and Eve lose the gift of the original goodness and immortality in which they were created and bring upon themselves

the sufferings of fruitless toil, pain in childbirth, and ulti-
mately, death itself.[8]

The Battle Between the "Serpent" and the "Woman"

Third, it is not just the man and the woman who are affected
by their sin. The real culprit, the serpent, is also punished.
In fact, part of the serpent's punishment involves a cryptic
oracle about a future battle between the offspring of the serpent and the offspring of the woman:

> The LORD God said to the serpent,
> "Because you have done this . . .
> *I will put enmity between you and the woman,*
> *and between your seed and her seed;*
> *he shall strike your head,*
> *and you shall strike his heel."*
> (Genesis 3:14–15)[9]

What are we to make of this mysterious oracle? On the one
hand, many modern commentators see it as simply a story
about the origin of the uneasy relationship between human
beings and snakes. On the other hand, as we will see in a moment, ancient Jewish interpreters saw it as referring to a spiritual battle between humanity and the Devil and his angels.
In support of this spiritual interpretation, it is worth noting
that in the very next chapter of Genesis, "sin" is described as
a beast "lurking at the door," waiting to strike at Cain, the
offspring of Eve. But he must "master" it (Genesis 4:1, 7).[10]

For our purposes here, what matters is that the oracle

describes *a future conflict between the serpent and the woman.*
When God declares that he will put "enmity" or "hostility"
between the serpent and the woman, the Hebrew word refers to lethal conflict between individuals (Numbers 35:21–
22) or war between peoples (see Ezekiel 25:15; 35:5). Indeed,
this war between the serpent and the woman will not stop;
the battle will continue between the "seed" or "offspring"
(Hebrew *zera'*) of both the serpent and the woman. In other
words, there are four parties involved in the battle:

The Battle in Genesis 3:15

1. The Serpent	versus	2. The Woman
3. Serpent's offspring (strikes the heel)	versus	4. Woman's offspring (crushes the head)

As anyone who has ever killed a snake knows, the safest
way to do so is to crush its head. At the same time, if you try
to step on its head, you take a fairly big risk of being struck
on the heel before killing it. When it comes to the oracle in
Genesis 3:15, the mysterious thing about the battle is that
both sides appear to lose: The serpent's offspring will "strike"
(Hebrew *suph*) the human's heel, and the woman's offspring
will "strike" (Hebrew *suph*) the serpent's head.

Eve in Ancient Jewish Tradition

Finally, before turning to the New Testament, we need to
take a brief look at what writings outside the Jewish Bible

have to say about Eve. Although these books are not considered inspired Scripture by Jews today (though two of them—
Wisdom and Sirach—were included in the Septuagint and
are part of the Catholic Old Testament), they are nonetheless
valuable witnesses to what many Jews living at the time of
Mary and Jesus would have believed. Several aspects of ancient Jewish traditions about Eve stand out as important.[11]

For one thing, although the book of Genesis itself simply refers to "the serpent" (Genesis 3:1), later Jewish writings
make clear that the one who tempts Eve is actually Satan.[12]
For example, the book of Wisdom states that it was "through
the devil's (Greek *diabolos*) envy that death entered the
world" (Wisdom 2:24). Likewise, another first-century Jewish interpretation says that "the devil" spoke to Eve "through
the mouth of the serpent" (*Life of Adam and Eve* 17:4).[13]

Moreover, ancient Jewish writings also affirm that the
effects of Adam and Eve's sin—sin and death—are trans-
mitted to all their descendants.[14] Consider the following examples, all from Jewish writings in circulation by the first
century:

> From a woman sin had its beginning, and *because of
> her we all die.* (Sirach 25:24)

> [God said:] "That man transgressed my ways and
> was persuaded by his wife; and she was deceived
> by the serpent. *And then death was ordained for the
> generations of men.*" (Pseudo-Philo, *Biblical Antiqui-
> ties,* 13:8)[15]

> O Adam, what have you done? For *though it was you*
> *who sinned, the fall was not yours alone, but ours also*
> *who are your descendants.* (4 Ezra 7:118)[16]

Clearly, around the time of Jesus, there was a widespread Jewish tradition that the Fall of Adam and Eve affected all human beings, even though their descendants were not personally guilty. In other words, these Jewish writings lay the foundations for what would later come to be known as the doctrine of "original sin."[17]

Finally, and most important of all, the oldest Jewish interpretations that we possess of the biblical oracle about the "serpent" and the "woman" (Genesis 3:15) saw it as a prophecy of *the Messiah.* The most significant example of this is the book of Enoch, which was very popular among Jews in the first century A.D. This ancient Jewish writing not only identifies the "Messiah" with the "Son of Man" (1 Enoch 48:2–10) but also links the Son of Man with the prophecy of the woman in Genesis 3:15:

> Pain shall seize them when they see that *Son of*
> *Man* sitting on the throne of his glory ... For *the*
> *offspring of the mother of the living* was concealed
> from the beginning (1 Enoch 62:5–7)[18]

What a remarkable passage! It shows us that already in the first century A.D., the Jewish Messiah was being identified with the "offspring" of Eve, the "mother of all living" (Genesis 3:15, 22). And this Jewish tradition did not stop in the first century. One ancient Jewish translation of Genesis into Aramaic (known as a Targum) also interprets the war between the woman and the serpent as a reference to the Messiah:

> I will put enmity between you and the woman and between your sons and her sons . . . For her sons, however, there will be a remedy, *but for you, O serpent, there will not be a remedy, since they are to make appeasement in the end, in the day of King Messiah.* (*Targum Neofiti* on Genesis 3:15)[19]

Although the exact date of this Targum continues to be debated,[20] for our purposes here, what matters is that it proves that ancient Christians were not the only ones who saw Genesis 3:15 as a Messianic prophecy. Ancient Jews did too. Thus, the Christian tradition of referring to Genesis 3:15 as the "First Gospel" (Latin *Protoevangelium*) is actually rooted in Jewish soil.[21]

To sum up, in ancient Jewish Scripture and tradition, Eve was no "ordinary woman." Not only did she play a crucial role in bringing sin and death into the world but it was one of her offspring—the Messiah—who was expected to rise up one day and undo the effects of the Fall. With this in mind, we can now turn and see what light these ancient Jewish beliefs about Eve can shine on the figure of Mary.

MARY THE NEW EVE

When we turn to the pages of the New Testament, we find Mary depicted in ways that echo the biblical portrait of Eve and the mysterious "woman" of Genesis 3:15. This happens in two books: the Gospel of John and the book of Revelation. Let's take a few moments to look carefully at each of them.

The Wedding at Cana and the "Woman" of Genesis

In the Gospel of John, Mary appears twice: once during the wedding at Cana (John 2:1–12), and once during the crucifixion of Jesus (John 19:25–27). When these two episodes are read alongside one another in light of ancient Jewish beliefs about Adam and Eve, they reveal clues that Mary is the "woman" of Genesis whose "offspring" will conquer the serpent (Genesis 3:15). Let's begin with the wedding at Cana:

> *On the third day there was a marriage at Cana in Galilee, and the mother of Jesus was there;* Jesus also was invited to the marriage, with his disciples. When the wine failed, the mother of Jesus said to him, "They have no wine." And Jesus said to her, *"Woman, what is that to you and to me? My hour has not yet come."* His mother said to the servants, "Do whatever he tells you." Now six stone jars were standing there, for the Jewish rites of purification, each holding twenty or thirty gallons. Jesus said to them, "Fill the jars with water." And they filled them up to the brim. He said to them, "Now draw some out, and take it to the steward of the feast." So they took it. When the steward of the feast tasted the water now become wine, and did not know where it came from (though the servants

who had drawn the water knew), the steward of the feast called the bridegroom and said to him, "Every man serves the good wine first; and when men have drunk freely, then the poor wine; but you have kept the good wine until now." This, *the first of his signs,* Jesus did at Cana in Galilee, and manifested his glory; and his disciples believed in him. (John 2:1–11)[22]

For our purposes here, two questions demand our attention. Why does the Gospel emphasize that the wedding at Cana took place on "the third day" (John 2:1)? And why does Jesus call Mary "Woman" (Greek *gynē*) (John 2:4)? We have no other examples of a Jewish man addressing his own mother this way.

At first glance, John's reference to "the third day" (John 2:1) might seem to be mere chronological information. However, when read in light of the entire chapter, it appears to be part of a series of allusions to the book of Genesis. Consider, for example, the very first line of John's Gospel:

The Book of Genesis	The Gospel of John
In the beginning God created the heavens and the earth . . . (Genesis 1:1)	*In the beginning* was the Word . . . and the Word was God. (John 1:1)

Just as Genesis begins with the famous account of the seven "days" of creation, the Gospel of John begins with the first seven "days" of Jesus' public ministry:

The Seven Days of the New Creation	
DAY 1	Testimony of John the Baptist (John 1:19)
DAY 2	"The next day" (John 1:29)—the Baptism of Jesus
DAY 3	"The next day" (John 1:35)—Jesus meets Andrew and Peter
DAY 4	"The next day" (John 1:43)—Jesus meets Philip and Nathanael
DAY 7	"The third day" [after Day 4] (John 2:1)—wedding at Cana

Notice here that the way scholars arrive at *seven* days is by interpreting John's references sequentially and adding the first four days to the "third day" (4 Days + 3 Days = 7 Days). In light of such parallels, both Protestant and Catholic commentators conclude that the Gospel of John is modeling the first seven days of Jesus' ministry on the first week of creation in Genesis.[23] John is depicting Jesus as a new Adam, whose public ministry is the beginning of "a new creation."

If this interpretation is correct, it provides a helpful explanation for why Jesus addresses his mother as "Woman" (Greek *gynē*) (John 2:4). Contrary to what some readers assume, he is *not* disrespecting Mary. As one Protestant scholar rightly insists: "By no means, however, does the translation of *gynē* as 'woman' imply . . . rudeness or hostility on the part of Jesus."[24] Instead, the most plausible explanation is that Jesus is addressing Mary as the "woman" of Genesis 3:15. In the words of Raymond Brown, in his influential commentary on the Gospel of John: *"John thinks of Mary against the background of Genesis 3 . . . Mary is the New Eve."*[25] In support of this interpretation, it's important to remember that in the book of Genesis, Eve is called "Eve" only once; she is called "woman" *eleven* times.[26] Thus, just as the first Eve invites the first Adam to commit the first sin, so now Mary invites Jesus to perform the first of his "signs."

This link between Mary and Eve is even stronger in John's account of Jesus' crucifixion and death. In order see it clearly, however, we need to keep in mind two points. First, in the Gospel of John, Jesus describes his death on the cross as the hour in which the Devil will be conquered:

> "Now is the judgment of this world, *now shall the ruler of this world be cast out.* And I, when I am lifted up from the earth, will draw all men to myself." He said this to show *by what death he was to die.* (John 12:31–33)

Second, at the very the hour when the Devil is finally defeated, Jesus once again addresses his own mother as "Woman":

> But standing by the cross of Jesus were *his mother,* and his mother's sister, Mary the wife of Clopas, and Mary Magdalene. When Jesus saw his mother, and the disciple whom he loved standing near, he said to his mother, *"Woman, behold, your son!"* Then he said to the disciple, "Behold, your mother!" And

from *that hour* the disciple took her to his own home. (John 19:25–27)

With this final piece of the puzzle in place, the parallels between Eve and Mary in the Gospel of John are complete:

Eve	Mary
1. Called "woman" (11 times)	1. Called "woman" (2 times)
2. Invites Adam to commit the first sin	2. Invites Jesus to perform his first sign
3. With Adam at the Fall; tempted by the Devil to sin	3. With Jesus at the crucifixion
4. Mother of the "offspring" who conquers the "serpent"	4. "Woman" whose "offspring" conquers the Devil
(Genesis 3:1–6, 15)	(John 2:1–12; 19:25–27)

In light of such parallels, there is good reason to conclude that in the Gospel of John, the mother of Jesus is no ordinary woman. In the words of New Testament scholar John Dominic Crossan: "Implicit in the title 'woman' is that her full destiny is to be *the 'woman' of Genesis 3:15.*"[27]

The Book of Revelation: The "Woman," the Serpent, and the Messiah

But the Gospel of John is not the only New Testament evidence for seeing Mary as foreshadowed in the book of

Genesis. Even more explicit is the vision of the "woman clothed with the sun" in the book of Revelation:

> And *a great portent* appeared in heaven, *a woman clothed with the sun,* with the moon under her feet, and on her head a crown of twelve stars; she was with child and she cried out in her pangs of birth, in anguish for delivery. And *another portent* appeared in heaven; behold, *a great red dragon,* with seven heads and ten horns, and seven diadems upon his heads. His tail swept down a third of the stars of heaven, and cast them to the earth. *And the dragon stood before the woman who was about to bear a child, that he might devour her child when she brought it forth; she brought forth a male child, one who is to rule all the nations with a rod of iron,* but her child was caught up to God and to his throne, and the woman fled into the wilderness, where she has a place prepared by God, in which to be nourished for one thousand two hundred and sixty days. Now war arose in heaven, Michael and his angels fighting against the dragon; and the dragon and his angels fought, but they were defeated and there was no longer any place for them in heaven. And *the great dragon* was thrown down, *that ancient serpent, who is called the Devil and Satan, the deceiver of the whole world*—he was thrown down to the earth, and his angels were thrown down with him . . . And when *the dragon* saw that he had been thrown down to the earth,

he pursued *the woman* who had borne the *male child*. (Revelation 12:1–9, 13)

Once again, a whole book could be written just on these verses.[28] I want to ask only one question: *Who is the woman clothed with the sun?* Is she an individual? Or does she symbolize a group of people?

On this point, scholars are divided. On the one hand, the woman can be seen as an individual.[29] For one thing, she is explicitly identified as the mother of the Messiah: She gives birth to the "male child" who is "to rule all the nations" (Revelation 12:5; compare Psalm 2:7–9). On the other hand, the woman can be interpreted as a collective figure—a symbol for the people of God.[30] One reason for seeing her this way is that in the Old Testament, Jerusalem is often depicted as the "bride" of God (Isaiah 62:1–6; Hosea 2:16) and the sufferings of the people to a "woman with child" who "cries out in her pangs" (Isaiah 26:17; Jeremiah 4:31–5:1; Micah 4:10). In fact, the book of Revelation describes the Church as the "Bride" of Christ and as a new "Jerusalem" (Revelation 19:7–8; 21:1–9). For these reasons, many interpreters conclude that the woman in John's vision is a symbol for Israel, or the Church, or both.

So what should we conclude? Is the woman an individual? Or is she a symbol for the people of God? In this case, the best explanation is not either/or but both/and. There are good reasons to conclude that the "woman clothed with the sun" is *both an individual figure and a symbol for the Church*. For one thing, scholars are virtually unanimous in recognizing that "the dragon" and the "male child" are primarily individual figures.[31] Look at it this way:

Three Individuals in Revelation 12			
1. The Serpent	=	the Devil	Individual (Satan)
2. The Child	=	the Messiah	Individual (Christ)
3. The Woman	=	Mother of the Messiah	Individual (Mary)

In other words, if the dragon symbolizes an individual (Satan), and the child symbolizes an individual (Jesus), then it makes sense that the woman also symbolizes an individual (Mary).

With that said, it's also important to stress that the serpent and the male child in Revelation 12 are not *merely* individuals. Like the woman, they are apocalyptic symbols for larger groups. For example, the dragon's "seven heads" and "ten horns" are explicitly identified later on in Revelation as "seven kings" and "ten kings" who persecute the followers of Christ (Revelation 17:7–14).[32] In a similar way, the child who is persecuted by the dragon also represents the "followers" of Jesus; that is why a few verses later they are called "the rest" of the woman's "offspring" (Revelation 12:17).[33] Now, if the dragon is an individual (Satan) who also represents a larger group (the wicked kings of the world), and the child is an individual (Jesus) who represents a larger group (the followers of Jesus), then it makes sense to conclude that the woman is also an individual (Mary) who represents a larger group (the Church). In the words of the Protestant biblical scholar Ben Witherington III:

> I would suggest . . . that this figure [the "woman"
> of Revelation 12] is both *the literal mother of the male
> child Jesus,* and also *the female image of the people of
> God.*[34]

In a similar way, the evangelical scholar Scot McKnight asks: "Is it possible that this woman is both Mary and the People of God?"[35] To my mind, the answer is a hearty Yes! That is why the most ancient Christian interpretations of Revelation 12 that we possess identify the woman clothed with the sun *both* with Mary *and* with the Church.[36]

In sum, according to the Gospel of John and the book of Revelation, Mary is not just the mother of Jesus. She is also a second Eve and the woman of Genesis 3:15, the mother of the Messiah whose offspring would conquer Satan and undo the Fall of Adam and Eve precisely by dying on the cross.

IMMACULATE MARY

Now that we've seen the New Testament parallels between Eve and Mary, we can begin to understand why ancient Christians came to believe that the mother of Jesus not only played a unique role in the history of salvation but also was preserved from all sin. We'll bring this chapter to a close by briefly looking at the connection between Mary's identity as the new Eve and the Catholic doctrine of her immaculate conception.[37]

Ancient Christians Everywhere: Mary Is the New Eve

First and foremost: Although many modern-day Christians are quick to insist that Mary was just an "ordinary woman," this was certainly not true of ancient Christians. In ancient times, the parallels between Eve and Mary were widely recognized and led to the recognition that just as Eve had played a unique role in the fall of humankind, so Mary plays a unique role in its redemption.[38] Consider the following quotations from ancient Christians living in the East and the West:

> For Eve . . . having conceived the word of the serpent, brought forth disobedience and death. But the Virgin Mary received faith and joy. (Justin Martyr, *Dialogue with Trypho* 100 [2nd century A.D.])[39]

> *The knot of Eve's disobedience was loosed by the obedience of Mary.* For what the virgin Eve had bound fast through unbelief, this did the virgin Mary set free through faith. (Irenaeus, *Against Heresies* 3.22.4 [2nd century A.D.])[40]

> Let women praise her, the pure Mary,—that as in Eve their mother,—great was their reproach,—lo! in Mary their sister,—greatly magnified was their honor. (Ephrem the Syrian, *Hymns on the Nativity* 15.23 [4th century A.D.])[41]

> Death came through a virgin, Eve. It was necessary that life also should come through a virgin . . . (Cyril of Jerusalem, *Catechetical Lectures* 12.15 [4th century A.D.])[42]

A maiden expelled us from paradise, through a maiden we find eternal life. (John Chrysostom, *Commentary on the Psalms* 45.4 [4th century A.D.])[43]

Death came through Eve, but life has come through Mary. (Jerome, *Letters* 22.21 [4th–5th century A.D.])[44]

Through woman, poison was poured upon man, in order to deceive him, but salvation was poured out upon man from a woman, that he might be reborn in grace. (Augustine, *Sermons* 51.3 [4th–5th century A.D.])[45]

What a remarkable symphony of ancient voices! Note well that these quotations are not from a few marginal writers limited to a particular place or time. They are from Christians writing in Greek, Latin, and Syriac, living in the Holy Land, Africa, Asia Minor, and Europe. For this reason, the famous nineteenth-century expert on the church fathers John Henry Newman once wrote: "The great rudimental teaching of Antiquity from the earliest date" about Mary is that "She is the Second Eve."[46]

The Creation of Eve and the Immaculate Conception

Eventually, the understanding of Mary as a second Eve led to the realization that Mary—like Eve herself—was created without sin.[47] The logic behind this belief is quite simple: *If Mary is really the new Eve, then she must be greater than Eve.*

If you think about it for a minute, this makes sense. It is a basic rule of Scripture that Old Testament prefigurations (known as "types") are never greater than their New Testament fulfillments. In the Bible, Adam prefigures Jesus, but Adam was not greater than Jesus (remember the Fall?). Likewise, David foreshadows Jesus, the true king of Israel. But David was certainly not greater than Christ (remember Bathsheba?). In the same way, if Eve foreshadows Mary, then she cannot be greater than Mary.

As we saw earlier, in the book of Genesis, Eve was created "very good"—that is, she was created without sin (Genesis 1:27–31). Therefore, it is reasonable to conclude that Mary, as the second Eve, must *also* have been created without sin. In fact, the Eve-Mary typology also suggests that Mary never committed a single sin. For if she had committed even one sin, then the *old* Eve would be greater than the *new* Eve. Just as Jesus, the new Adam, was created without sin and lived free from sin, so too Mary, the new Eve, was free from sin. Consider the words of the ancient Christian writers Ephrem the Syrian and Augustine of Hippo:

> Only you [Jesus] and your Mother are more beautiful than everything. *For on you, O Lord, there is no mark; neither is there any stain in your Mother.* (Ephrem, *Nisibene Hymns* 27.8 [4th century A.D.])[48]

> *We must except the holy Virgin Mary, concerning whom I wish to raise no question when it touches the subject of sins,* out of honor to the Lord; for from Him we know what *abundance of grace* for overcoming sin

in every particular was *conferred upon her* who had
the merit to conceive and bear Him who undoubt-
edly had no sin. (Augustine, *On Nature and Grace*
42 [4th–5th century A.D.])[49]

Notice here that both Ephrem and Augustine recognize that,
apart from Jesus himself, Mary is the only "exception" to the
biblical teaching that all human beings after the Fall are born
under the power of sin (see Psalm 51:5; Romans 3:23, 5:12–
17). Notice also that Augustine is very explicit that Mary's
freedom from sin is not the result of her own efforts. It is not
something she earns but is a *pure gift* of God's "grace."

Nevertheless, the question remains: How can ancient
Christians say such things about Mary? The New Testament
clearly says that Jesus was without sin (Hebrews 4:15). But
how can we add Mary to the list? Wouldn't Mary's being
created without sin mean that she was somehow less than
fully human? *Not unless Adam and Eve before the Fall are also
"less than fully human."*[50] Remember: We have to look at Jesus
and Mary from an ancient *Jewish* perspective. And in the
Jewish Bible, God does not create Adam and Eve in a state of
sin but "very good" (Genesis 1:31). Thus, it makes sense that
he would also create the new Adam and Eve without sin:

Old Testament	New Testament
1. Adam: created without sin	1. Jesus: conceived without sin
2. Eve: created without sin	2. Mary: conceived without sin

In sum: If Adam is created without sin, and Eve is created without sin, then why can't both Jesus *and Mary* also be conceived without sin? If Jesus really is the new Adam and Mary really is the second Eve, then it is fitting that *both* of them would be free from sin, without in any way jeopardizing the fullness of their humanity.[51]

In fact, it is precisely Jesus' and Mary's identities as the new Adam and the new Eve that are cited by the official *Catechism of the Catholic Church* as the biblical foundation for the doctrine that Mary was conceived without sin and that she remained free from sin her whole life. In its discussion of Genesis 3:15 as the "First Gospel" (Latin *Protoevangelium*), the Catechism says this:

> The Christian tradition sees in [Genesis 3:15] an announcement of *the "New Adam"* who, because he "became obedient unto death, even death on a cross," makes amends superabundantly for the disobedience of Adam. Furthermore many Fathers and Doctors of the Church have seen the woman announced in the Protoevangelium as Mary, the mother of Christ, *the "new Eve."* Mary benefited first of all and uniquely from Christ's victory over sin: *she was preserved from all stain of original sin and by a special grace of God committed no sin of any kind during her whole earthly life.* (CCC 411)

Notice here that Mary's preservation from original sin—known as the "immaculate conception"—has nothing to do with the sinlessness of her parents (as is sometimes wrongly believed). Nor does it have anything to do with Mary being "cleansed so she would not pass on a sinful nature to her son," as one Protestant scholar recently claimed.[52] Instead, according to Catholic teaching, Mary's freedom from any personal sin is the result of a "special grace" that flows directly from Jesus' victory over sin. It is not something she earns through her own power. When Pope Pius IX formally defined the dogma of the immaculate conception in 1854, he followed ancient Christian belief in emphasizing that Mary's preservation from all stain of original sin took place by "a singular grace" of God and "by virtue of the merits of Jesus Christ" (Pius IX, *Ineffabilis Deus*).[53] For this reason, despite her sinlessness—or rather, precisely *because* she was preserved from all sin—Mary can truly declare that "God" is her "Savior" (Luke 1:47).

Mary: The Beginning of the New Creation

In conclusion, as the new Eve, Mary is the supreme example of what God's grace can do in a mere human creature. She helps us see clearly that the "good news" of salvation is about undoing the effects of the fall of Adam and Eve and becoming a "new creation" in Christ (2 Corinthians 5:17). She helps us to understand that not only did Jesus live without sin on this earth but also, through God's grace, in the resurrection *we too* can be completely free from sin. That is why the New Testament itself describes the "spirits" of "just men" who are in heaven as being "made perfect" (Hebrews 12:23). Christ did not die on the cross so that God could pretend that we are righteous. According to Paul, God will truly "make" *us* "righteous" through the power of his grace (Romans 5:19). As the new Eve, Mary is created without sin to be a "living sign" of the righteous life of the new creation that is ushered in by Jesus' life, death, and resurrection from the dead. As Jesus himself says in the book of Revelation: "Behold, I make all things new" (Revelation 21:5).[54]

Of course, Eve is not the only figure in the Jewish Bible that points forward to Mary. Even more enigmatic is the next key to unlocking the mysteries of Jesus' mother: the lost Ark of the Covenant.

chapter 3

THE NEW ARK

◇◇◇◇◇

My first encounter with the Ark of the Covenant was through the blockbuster movie *Raiders of the Lost Ark*. Since I was too young to see the film when it was first released, I got a Read-Along Book and Record version for Christmas. I still vividly remember one of its pictures: Professor Indiana Jones holding open a dusty old Bible and pointing to a drawing of the Israelites conquering their enemies by means of the sacred chest and its "mysterious powers." According to Professor Jones, any army who carried the Ark into battle was undefeatable.

Looking back now, I can't help but wonder what impact that book had on my later fascination with the Bible and archaeology (and my decision to become a professor). In any case, I was much older when I learned that the premise for the film—the "lost" Ark of the Covenant—is actually deeply rooted in Jewish Scripture and tradition. Although there was a thriving Temple in Jerusalem at the time of Jesus, from a Jewish point of view, this Temple was missing something essential. The Holy of Holies, which was supposed to house the Ark of the Covenant, was *empty*. Nevertheless, as we will see momentarily, there was a Jewish tradition that the location of the lost Ark would one day be revealed.

One reason this ancient Jewish hope for the return of the Ark is important is that, according to the New Testament, Jesus is not just the new Adam. He is also the *new Moses*, who has come to inaugurate a *new exodus*. Over and over again, Jesus does and says things strikingly similar to what Moses did and said. Just as Moses fasted for forty days and forty nights on Mount Sinai (Exodus 34:28), so Jesus fasts for forty days and forty nights in the desert (Luke 4:1–2). Just as Moses fed the Israelites in the desert with miraculous bread from heaven (Exodus 16:1–31), so Jesus feeds the multitudes in the wilderness with miraculous bread (Luke 9:10–17). And just as Moses established the "covenant" with the twelve tribes of Israel (Exodus 24:1–8), so Jesus establishes a "new covenant" with the twelve apostles at the Last Supper (Luke 22:20).

On the other hand, the exodus inaugurated by Jesus is also strikingly different from the exodus from Egypt at the time of Moses. Perhaps the most significant difference has to do with *where* the new exodus begins and ends. The word "exodus" means "journey." With every journey, there must be a point of departure and a destination. For Moses, the exodus begins in the land of Egypt and ends in the promised land. According to the Gospel of Luke, however, the exodus of Jesus is different:

And behold, two men talked with [Jesus], Moses and Elijah, who appeared in glory and spoke of *his departure* (Greek *exodos*), *which he was to accomplish at Jerusalem*. (Luke 9:30–31)

Then [after the resurrection] ... lifting up his hands he blessed them. While he blessed them, *he parted from them, and was carried up into heaven*. (Luke 24:50–51)

For Luke, the new exodus begins in *Jerusalem* and ends in *heaven*. In contrast to the journey of Moses, for Jesus the earthly promised land is just the point of departure—not the ultimate destination.

The reason all of this matters for us is this: *If Jesus is the new Moses, then where is the new Ark?* As any first-century Jew would have known, during the time of the first exodus, the Ark of the Covenant played a central role. Thus, if the Messiah was to be a new Moses who inaugurated a new exodus, then it would make sense for him to bring back the lost Ark of the Covenant. How can you have a new exodus without a new Ark?

In this chapter, we will explore how the New Testament reveals that *Mary is the new Ark* of the new exodus. As we will see, Mary's identity as the new Ark has direct implications for ancient Christian beliefs about the divinity of Jesus as well as the bodily assumption of Mary into heaven at the end of her life. In order to see all this clearly, however, we have to go back and do a bit of digging into what happened to the original Ark.

THE LOST ARK OF THE COVENANT

In order to get a firm grasp on ancient Jewish beliefs about the return of the lost Ark, we need to start with the Hebrew Bible.[1] Then, once we've clarified the biblical accounts of the Ark, we can take a few moments to explore what later Jewish writings have to say.

The Ark of the Covenant: Dwelling Place of God on Earth

The first time the Ark of the Covenant is mentioned in Jewish Scripture is in the book of Exodus, in the midst of the story of Israel's departure from Egypt and their forty-year journey through the desert. After the people of Israel arrive at Mount Sinai and receive the Ten Commandments (Exodus 19–20), God does something extremely significant. He gives the Israelites instructions for how to build a sanctuary for him to dwell in—a kind of portable temple, known as the "Tabernacle" (Exodus 25:8–9).

The very first piece of sacred furniture that God commands to be built and placed in the Tabernacle is the Ark of the Covenant. Although it is detailed, the initial description of the Ark is worth reading carefully:

> And *let them make me a sanctuary, that I may dwell in their midst.* According to all that I show you concerning the pattern of *the tabernacle,* and of all its furniture, so you shall make it. They shall make *an ark of acacia wood* . . . And *you shall overlay it with pure gold,* within and without shall you

overlay it . . . You shall make poles of acacia wood, and overlay them with gold. And you shall put the poles into the rings on the sides of the ark, to carry the ark by them . . . *And you shall put into the ark the testimony which I shall give you.* Then you shall make a mercy seat of pure gold . . . And *you shall make two cherubim of gold;* of hammered work shall you make them, on the two ends of the mercy seat . . . The cherubim shall spread out their wings above, overshadowing the mercy seat with their wings, their faces one to another; toward the mercy seat shall the faces of the cherubim be. And you shall put the mercy seat on the top of the ark; and in the ark you shall put the testimony that I shall give you. *There I will meet with you, and from above the mercy seat,* from between the two cherubim that are upon the ark of the testimony, *I will speak with you* of all that I will give you in commandment for the people of Israel. (Exodus 25:8–14, 16–18, 20–22)

For our purposes here, several features of the Ark are important to highlight.[2]

First and foremost, the Tabernacle where the Ark is kept is the *dwelling place of God on earth.* That's the reason the "sanctuary" is built: to be the place where God will "dwell" in the "midst" of his people (Exodus 25:8).[3] Inside the Tabernacle, the Ark will be where God will "meet with" his people and "speak" to them (Exodus 25:22).

Second, the Ark is a sacred chest containing the Ten

Commandments. That is what God means when he says: "You shall put into the ark the testimony which I shall give you" (Exodus 25:16). The Hebrew word for "ark" (Hebrew *'aron*) simply means "box" or "chest," and the word "testimony" is another way of referring to the tablets of the Ten Commandments (Exodus 31:18). Eventually, in addition to the two tablets, a golden bowl of manna and the miraculous staff of the high priest Aaron that "budded" would also be kept inside the Ark (see Exodus 16:34; Numbers 17:10).[4]

Third, the Ark is made of *incorruptible wood*. God is very specific that the Ark shall be made of "acacia wood" (Hebrew *shittim*). As Old Testament scholars point out, acacia wood was regarded as holy in ancient Egypt; it is also extremely durable.[5] In fact, the Jewish Septuagint translates "acacia" as "incorruptible wood" (Exodus 25:5 LXX).[6] Likewise, the first-century Jewish historian Josephus wrote that the Ark was made "of wood that was naturally strong, and could not be corrupted" (Josephus, *Antiquities* 3.134).[7]

Fourth, the Ark is covered in pure gold. In the Jewish Bible, the word "pure" (Hebrew *tahor*) is used to refer to gold that is "clean"—that is, free from any impurities.[8] In context, the purity of the gold used seems to symbolize the *absolute holiness of the Ark*.[9] That is why it can be carried only using the golden poles; the Ark is too holy for sinful human beings even to touch it. For readers who might assume that all statues are unbiblical, it is important to point out here that God himself commands the Israelites to make two *golden statues* of "cherubim"—that is, angels—and place them on top of the Ark (Exodus 25:17–18). It is also worth noting that the holiness of the Ark is also clear from the fact that elsewhere in

Scripture the Israelites are commanded to "cover the ark" by veiling it with "a cloth of blue," whenever they have to carry it (Numbers 4:5–6).

Finally, the Ark and the Tabernacle together are the *place where the glory "cloud" will descend from heaven.*[10] When Moses and the Israelites finally finish building the Tabernacle and put the Ark inside, this is what happens:

> [Moses] brought the ark into the tabernacle... So Moses finished the work. *Then the cloud covered the tent of meeting, and the glory of the LORD filled the tabernacle. And Moses was not able to enter the tent of meeting, because the cloud abode upon it, and the glory of the LORD filled the tabernacle.* Throughout all their journeys, whenever the cloud was taken up from over the tabernacle, the people of Israel would go onward; but if the cloud was not taken up, then they did not go onward till the day that it was taken up. (Exodus 40:21, 33–38)

It is difficult to overestimate the significance of the descent of the cloud of God's "glory" (Hebrew *kabod*) upon the Tabernacle. The glory cloud was not just a visible sign that God had come down to earth to be with his people. It was also the means by which God would lead his people through the wilderness to bring them home to the promised land. As a rule, if the Israelites fought their enemies with the Ark in their midst, they were victorious (Joshua 6:1–21), but if the Ark was absent, they were defeated (Numbers 14:44–45; compare, however, 1 Samuel 4).

The Ark Goes Up to Jerusalem

For many people, the familiar tale of the Ark stops with the book of Exodus. But according to the Bible, there is much more to be said.

To make a long story very short: Once the Israelites arrive in the promised land of Canaan, the Ark of the Covenant moves around quite a bit.[11] During the time of Joshua and the Judges of Israel (traditionally dated between 1450 and 1020 B.C.), the Ark is kept at various local sanctuaries in the promised land, such as Gilgal, Shiloh, and Bethel (see Joshua 4:19, 7:6, 18:1; Judges 20:26–28). At one point, the Ark is actually captured by the Philistines, until they are stricken by God with a plague of "tumors"—which the New American Bible translates as a plague of "hemorrhoids" (1 Samuel 5:1–12)! In the face of this kind of suffering, it's understandable that the Philistines quickly return the Ark to the Israelites (1 Samuel 6:1–7:3).

Eventually, sometime around 1000 B.C., King David decides to bring the Ark from Baale-judah to the city of Jerusalem and give it a permanent home. According to the second book of Samuel, David "arose and went" with the people of Israel "to bring up . . . the ark of God" (2 Samuel 6:1–2). Tragically, instead of carrying the Ark with the golden poles (as the Law of Moses instructed), they placed the Ark upon a cart of oxen—a plan which proves fatal for a man named Uzzah:

> And when they came to the threshing floor of
> Nacon, Uzzah put out his hand to the ark of God
> and took hold of it, for the oxen stumbled. And the

anger of the LORD was kindled against Uzzah; and God smote him there because he put forth his hand to the ark; and he died there beside the ark of God. And David was angry because the LORD had broken forth upon Uzzah . . . *And David was afraid of the LORD that day; and he said, "How can the ark of the LORD come to me?"* So David was not willing to take the ark of the LORD into the city of David; but David took it aside to the house of Obed-edom the Gittite. And the ark of the LORD remained in the house of Obed-edom the Gittite three months; and the LORD blessed Obed-edom and all his household. (2 Samuel 6:6–11)

Once David discovers that Obed-edom and his family are actually blessed "because of the ark of God," he resumes bringing the Ark up to Jerusalem (2 Samuel 6:12). This time, they do it the right way, carrying the Ark by its poles and offering sacrifices of thanksgiving to God: "So David went and brought up the ark of God from the house of Obed-edom to the city of David with rejoicing . . . And David danced before the LORD with all his might . . . So David and all the house of Israel brought up the ark of the LORD with shouting, and with the sound of the horn" (2 Samuel 6:12, 14–15).

Although for many people today, the bringing of the Ark to Jerusalem by King David is not one of the most familiar passages in the Bible, the same was not true for ancient Jews. For them, the ascent of King David and the Ark to the mountain of Jerusalem was nothing less than the coming of God himself.[12] The event is memorialized in one of the Psalms "of

Ascents" that Jewish pilgrims would sing while "going up" to Jerusalem:[13]

> *Remember, O LORD, in David's favor,* all the hardships
>   he endured;
> how he swore to the LORD and vowed to the Mighty
>   One of Jacob,
> "I will not enter my house or get into my bed;
> I will not give sleep to my eyes or slumber to my
>   eyelids,
> until I find a place for the LORD,
> a dwelling place for the Mighty One of Jacob . . ."
> *Arise, O LORD, and go to your resting place,*
> *you and the ark of your might.*
> Let your priests be clothed with righteousness,
> and let your saints shout for joy . . .
> *For the LORD has chosen Zion;* he has desired it for his
>   habitation:
> *"This is my resting place for ever; here I will dwell."*
> (Psalm 132:1–5, 8–9, 13–14)[14]

Notice here that for the Psalmist, where the Ark goes, the presence of "the LORD" goes. Why? Because of the glory cloud. Likewise, when we turn to the biblical account of King Solomon finishing the building of the Jerusalem Temple, we discover that it is only after the priests bring the Ark of the Covenant into the Holy of Holies that the "cloud" from heaven once again comes down and fills the Temple (1 Kings 8:10–11). Now that the Ark is where it belongs, God can once again dwell with his people.[15]

Unfortunately, after the death of Solomon, the whole thing fell apart. Not only did the kingdom of Israel eventually split in two (see 1 Kings 11–12), but eventually, the Temple itself and the city of Jerusalem were destroyed. According to the prophet Ezekiel, before the Temple was destroyed by the Babylonians (in 587 B.C.), the "glory" cloud of God's presence departed from Jerusalem (Ezekiel 10).

What Happened to the Lost Ark of the Covenant?

So what actually happened to the Ark of the Covenant? How was it lost?

As anyone who has watched one of the many television documentaries about the "mysteries of the Bible" knows, theories about the location of the lost Ark abound.[16] Some assume that the Ark was stolen by the Babylonians when they destroyed the Temple. However, the Hebrew Scriptures themselves do not list the Ark among the sacred objects that were taken by Babylon (see 2 Kings 25:13–17; Jeremiah 52:17–23). Others speculate that the Ark is hidden is some unknown location, just waiting to be discovered by some lucky archaeologist (like Indiana Jones). One popular theory holds that the Ark is currently hidden in Ethiopia in a sanctuary that can be entered only by the monks who guard it, thus making it impossible for outsiders to verify or falsify the claim.

The odd thing about all of these theories is that they ignore the oldest evidence we possess regarding the disappearance of the Ark. I am referring to the ancient Jewish tradition that the prophet Jeremiah took the Ark from Jerusalem and hid it in Mount Nebo, in the territory east of the Jordan River, shortly before the Temple was destroyed. This important tradition is preserved in 2 Maccabees, usually dated to the mid-second century B.C.:

> It was also in the writing that *the prophet [Jeremiah]*, having received an oracle, *ordered that the tent and the ark should follow with him*, and that *he went out to the mountain where Moses had gone up and had seen the inheritance of God*. And Jeremiah came and found a cave, and he brought there the tent and the ark and the altar of incense, and he sealed up the entrance. Some of those who followed him came up to mark the way, but could not find it. When Jeremiah learned of it, he rebuked them and declared: *"The place shall be unknown until God gathers his people together again and shows his mercy. And then the Lord will disclose these things, and the glory of the Lord and the cloud will appear, as they were shown in the case of Moses*, and as Solomon asked that the place should be specially consecrated." (2 Maccabees 2:4–8)

Although this fascinating tradition is well known to scholars, it is not familiar to many Bible readers, because it is found only in the Catholic Old Testament. According to 2 Maccabees, there is no mystery about the fate of the Ark. We know exactly what happened to it. Jeremiah the prophet, who was also a priest in the Jerusalem Temple, hid the Ark in a cave on Mount Nebo—the same mountain where Moses had been allowed by God to go up and see the promised land before he died (Deuteronomy 34:1–4).[17] On the other hand, the text also reflects the ancient Jewish belief that one day, *the lost Ark will reappear.* When will the Ark be found? According to Jeremiah, its location shall remain "unknown" until God "shows his mercy" and brings back the glory "cloud" (2 Maccabees 2:8). In other words, you will know where the Ark is when you see it overshadowed by the cloud of "the glory of the Lord."

One reason this tradition is so significant is that at the time of Jesus, the Jewish people were still waiting for the return of the lost Ark. Although modern-day readers are often unaware, first-century Jews knew full well that the current Jerusalem Temple was lacking two crucially important features. First, it was missing the glory cloud, which had departed from the Temple shortly before it was destroyed by Babylon (see Ezekiel 10:18–22, 11:22–23). Second, and equally devastating, it was missing the Ark. In the words of the first-century Jewish historian Josephus:

> But the inmost part of the temple . . . was also separated from the outer part by a veil. *In this there was nothing at all.* It was inaccessible and inviolable, and not to be seen by any; and was called the Holy of Holies. (Josephus, *War* 5.219)[18]

Remarkably, Josephus's words find confirmation in the Greco-Roman histories of Tacitus, who tells us that when the Roman general Pompey conquered Jerusalem in the first century B.C., he actually went inside the Jerusalem Temple but found that "the place was empty and the secret shrine contained nothing" (Tacitus, *Histories* 5.9).[19]

In short, at the time of Jesus, any Jew familiar with Scripture and tradition would have known that the Jewish people were not only waiting for a new Moses to come and deliver them. They were also waiting for the revelation of the location of the Ark and the return of the glory cloud of God's presence. With these two hopes in mind, we can now turn to what the New Testament reveals about the location of the lost Ark and the revelation of God's glory.

MARY THE NEW ARK

When we turn to the pages of the New Testament and read them through ancient Jewish eyes, conscious of the importance of a new exodus and the Ark of the Covenant, we discover that Mary, the mother of Jesus, is linked with the glory cloud and the Ark itself. We find this in the Gospel of Luke and the book of Revelation. Let's take a few moments to examine the evidence.

The Annunciation: The Return of the Glory Cloud

The first key passage for connecting Mary with the Ark of the Covenant is the famous account of the annunciation: The angel Gabriel appears to the virgin Mary and announces that she will miraculously conceive and give birth to Jesus (Luke 1:26–38). For most readers, the main point of this account is that Gabriel is announcing the conception of the "Son of the Most High" (Luke 1:32). And this is certainly right.

However, from a first-century Jewish perspective, the annunciation is not just the story of the conception of "the Son of God" (Luke 1:35). It is also the story of the return of the long-absent "cloud" of God's "glory." You can see this if you look carefully at Gabriel's words to Mary. After the angel announces that she will conceive and bear a son, Mary responds by asking: "How shall this be, since I do not know man?" (Luke 1:34). We'll come back to the meaning of these words in Chapter 5. For now, what matters is Gabriel's response to Mary's question:

> And the angel said to her,
> *"The Holy Spirit will come upon you,*
> and *the power of the Most High will overshadow you;*
> therefore the child to be born will be called holy,
> the Son of God. (Luke 1:35)

There it is. Did you catch the image of the "glory cloud" from the Old Testament? Although it's easy to miss in the English translation, when you compare the original Greek of Luke's account with the ancient Jewish translation known as the Septuagint (commonly referred to as the "LXX"), you'll discover an important parallel between the descent of the *glory cloud* upon the Tabernacle and the descent of the *Holy Spirit* upon Mary:

The Tabernacle	The Virgin Mary
The cloud of the Lord's glory "overshadows" (*episkiazō*) the Tabernacle. (Exodus 40:35–35 LXX)	The Holy Spirit "overshadows" (*episkiazō*) the Virgin Mary. (Luke 1:35)

In light of the distinctive use of the word "overshadow" (Greek *episkiazō*) in the Greek Bible, many scholars from a variety of perspectives—Jewish, Protestant, and Catholic—have concluded that the imagery of the Holy Spirit overshadowing Mary is meant to call to mind the "glory cloud" of the exodus.[20] As one Protestant scholar writes:

> Mary's experience is to be compared with the dramatic way in which God's glory and the cloud marking his presence came down upon the completed tabernacle.[21]

In other words, just as the Ark in the Tabernacle was the special place of God's presence in the exodus from Egypt, so now, through the annunciation Mary has become the special dwelling place of God's glory in the new exodus.

The Visitation to Elizabeth: The New Ark Revealed

Significantly, these allusions to the Tabernacle and the Ark do not stop with Luke's account of the annunciation. Several more striking parallels between Mary and the Ark are present in Luke's account of Mary's visitation to her cousin Elizabeth (Luke 1:39–56). For most readers, the main point of the visitation is to tell how John the Baptist "leaped for joy" in his mother's womb (Luke 1:44). However, when we re-read the account of the visitation in light of what the Jewish Scriptures say about the Ark of the Covenant, we discover that something more is going on:

In those days Mary arose and went with haste into the hill country, to a city of Judah, and she entered the house of Zechariah and greeted Elizabeth. And when Elizabeth heard the greeting of Mary, the babe leaped in her womb; and Elizabeth was filled with the Holy Spirit *and she exclaimed with a loud cry,* "Blessed are you among women, and blessed is the fruit of your womb! *And why is this granted me, that the mother of my Lord should come to me?* For behold, when the voice of your greeting came to my ears, *the babe in my womb leaped for joy.* And blessed is she who believed that there would be a fulfillment of what was spoken to her from the Lord." And Mary said, "My soul magnifies the Lord, and my spirit rejoices in God my Savior, for he has regarded the low estate of his handmaiden. For behold, henceforth all generations will call me blessed; for he who is mighty has done great things for me, and holy is his name . . . *He has helped his servant Israel, in remembrance of his mercy,* as he spoke to our fathers, to Abraham and to his posterity for ever." *And Mary remained with her about three months,* and returned to her home. (Luke 1:39–49, 54–56)

When Luke's account of Mary's visit to Elizabeth is read in light of the Old Testament story of David bringing the Ark up to Jerusalem, several striking parallels emerge:

The Ark of the Covenant	The Virgin Mary
The glory of the Lord and the cloud cover the Tabernacle (containing the Ark) and *"overshadow"* (*episkiazō*) them. (Exodus 40:34–35, cf. v. 3)	The Holy Spirit comes upon Mary and the power of the Most High *"over-shadows"* (*episkiazō*) her. (Luke 1:35)
David *"arose and went"* to the hill country of *Judah* to bring up "the ark of God." (2 Samuel 6:2)	Mary *"arose and went"* into the hill country of *Judah* to visit Elizabeth. (Luke 1:39)
David admits his unworthi-ness to receive the Ark by exclaiming: "How can *the ark of the LORD come to me?"* (2 Samuel 6:9)	Elizabeth admits her unworthiness to receive Mary by exclaiming: "And why is this granted to me, that *the mother of my Lord* should *come to me?"* (Luke 1:43)
David *"leaped"* before the Ark as it was brought in *"with shouting."* (2 Samuel 6:15–16)	John *"leaped"* in Elizabeth's womb at the sound of Mary's voice and Elizabeth cried *"with a loud shout."* (Luke 1:41–42)
The Ark remained in the hill country, in the house of Obed-Edom, *"three months."* (2 Samuel 6:11)	Mary remained in the hill country, in Elizabeth's house, *"three months."* (Luke 1:56)

How do we explain these parallels between Mary and the Ark? Are they just coincidences?

Unfortunately, many books and commentaries simply *ignore* the parallels between Mary and the Ark, as if they do not exist.[22] Others acknowledge that the parallels are present, but fail to provide a plausible explanation for their existence.[23] Still others, after picking out one parallel and dismissing it as too "subtle," proceed as if they have explained away the presence of all of the parallels.[24]

In my opinion, none of these approaches is convincing. Instead, the most plausible explanation is also the simplest: In both the annunciation and the visitation, Luke is depicting Mary as the new Ark.[25] In the words of the Protestant scholar Max Thurian:

> One might further relate the account of Mary's visitation to Elizabeth with the account of the bearing of the Ark of the covenant by David . . . She has seen Mary the one who bears the Holy Presence, and she cannot withhold the great cry of ecstasy which characterized the appearance of the Ark as the place of the Lord's Presence.[26]

In support of this conclusion, it's important to remember (as we just saw) that many scholars recognize the parallel between the annunciation to Mary and the descent of the "glory cloud" upon the Tabernacle. If this is correct, then the presence of allusions to the Ark in the account of the visitation is perfectly consistent with Luke's earlier depiction of Mary. Moreover, the intention to reveal Mary as the new

Ark would explain why Luke rather curiously says Mary stayed with Elizabeth for "three months" (Luke 1:56). Why doesn't Luke just say Mary stayed "until the birth of John"? The best explanation for this chronological detail is that Luke is subtly but deliberately alluding to the story of the Ark staying in the house of Obed-Edom for "three months" (2 Samuel 6:11).[27]

In short, just as Luke portrays Jesus as the new Moses who will bring about the new exodus, so too Mary is being revealed as the new Ark—the new dwelling place of God's presence on earth.

The Book of Revelation: The Ark and the Woman in Heaven

Finally, the Gospel of Luke is not the only New Testament book that forges a link between Mary and the Ark of the Covenant. Something similar takes place in the book of Revelation.

I am referring once again to John's famous vision of the "woman clothed with the sun" (Revelation 12:1–2). As we saw in Chapter 2, there are solid reasons for concluding that the woman in Revelation 12 is the mother of the Messiah. What I did not point out in that chapter is that there is also a close connection between the woman and the lost Ark. You can see this connection by backing up a few verses and putting the vision of the woman in context:

> Then God's temple in heaven was opened, and *the ark of his covenant appeared within his temple;* and

there were flashes of lightning, voices, peals of thunder, an earthquake, and heavy hail. And *a great portent appeared in heaven, a woman clothed with the sun,* with the moon under her feet, and on her head a crown of twelve stars; she was with child and she cried out in her pangs of birth, in anguish for delivery. (Revelation 11:19–12:2)[28]

Notice three things about this mysterious passage.

First, although most English translations insert a "chapter" break between the appearance of the Ark and the appearance of the woman, no such division exists in the original Greek text. The contemporary system of chapters and verses was not added to the Bible until the thirteenth century by the Catholic archbishop of Canterbury Stephen Langton.[29] Hence, as experts on Revelation agree, the verse in which the Ark appears is not the *end* of the previous chapter but the *beginning* of a new section: It "introduces" the vision in which the woman appears.[30]

Second, both the Ark and the woman appear to be *in the heavenly Temple.* Notice the imagery of "noises" or "voices" (Greek *phōnai*) coming from the heavenly "temple" and a woman "in anguish for delivery" (Revelation 11:19, 12:2). These images are taken directly from the book of Isaiah: "A voice from the temple! The voice of the LORD, rendering recompense to his enemies! Before she was in labor she gave birth; before her pain came upon her she was delivered of a son" (Isaiah 66:6–7). We'll come back to this remarkable prophecy later in the book. For now, the main point is that it strongly suggests that Revelation is situating both the

Ark and the woman in the heavenly Temple. One reason this matters is that, as one New Testament scholar writes: "The presence of the ark of the covenant in the heavenly temple implies that it is the 'true' ark."[31] No first-century Jew who was waiting for the return of the lost Ark could read this vision in Revelation without being stunned that the true Ark was no longer on earth but in heaven.

Third and finally, the heavenly Ark is being associated with the heavenly woman. As the Protestant New Testament scholar Craig Koester points out in his commentary on Revelation, the repetition of the word "appeared" (Greek *ōphthē*) clearly "links the manifestation of the Ark" to the vision of the woman in the very next verse. Just as the Ark "appears" in heaven, so too the woman "appears" in heaven (Revelation 11:19, 12:1).[32]

What are the implications of all these observations? Although Revelation does not explicitly refer to Mary as the true Ark, the fact that it describes the Ark and the woman so close to one another is remarkable. At the very least, it implies that the woman (the mother of the Messiah) is in the same place the true Ark is—the heavenly Holy of Holies. Even more, it implies that for John, the woman and the Ark are *dual symbols* for the same person. This makes sense given John's love for dual symbols: Just as the "dragon" and the "serpent" are dual symbols for "the Devil" (Revelation 12:3, 9), and the "male child" and "the Lamb" are dual symbols for Christ (Revelation 12:5, 11), so the "Ark" and the "woman" are dual symbols for Mary, the mother of the Messiah (Revelation 11:19, 12:1). That, at least, is how the ninth-century Christian author Paschasius Radbertus interpreted the book of Revelation when he wrote: "The temple of God was open and the Ark of the Covenant was seen. *This certainly was not the Ark made by Moses, but is the Blessed Virgin . . ."*[33]

ASSUMED INTO HEAVEN

Now that we have studied ancient Jewish beliefs about the Ark of the Covenant as well as the New Testament parallels between Mary and the Ark, we can bring this chapter to a close by drawing out three important theological implications from what we've learned.

Mary's Body: The Dwelling Place of God on Earth

First and foremost, if Mary is the new Ark, then her body is nothing less than *the dwelling place of God on earth.*

Think about it. The old Ark was made of "pure gold" and kept in the "Holy of Holies" because it was "the place" where God would descend from heaven to "meet" his people. It was the sacred container for the Ten Commandments, the manna from heaven, and the staff of Aaron (Hebrews 9:4). So now the new and greater Ark must likewise be free from any impurity and completely holy. Mary is the sacred vessel for the "Word" made flesh, the "Bread of Life," and the true "high priest":

The Ark of the Covenant	Mary, the New Ark
1. Ten Commandments	1. "Word" made "Flesh"
2. Golden Urn of Manna	2. "Bread of Life" from Heaven
3. Staff of Aaron that Budded (Hebrews 9:4)	3. Heavenly "High Priest" (John 1:14, 6:53–58)

Now, if Mary is the new Ark, and the Ark is the dwelling place of God on earth, then, by implication, Jesus is God on earth. In other words, he is divine. The mystery of Mary's identity as the new Ark illuminates the even deeper mystery of Jesus' divinity.

And I'm not the first one to see this. The link between Mary and the Ark and the divinity of Christ was noticed by Christians writing long ago. Consider the words of ancient Christians writing in Rome, Egypt, and Syria:

> The Lord was made without sin, made in His human nature of *incorruptible wood, that is to say, of the Virgin and the Holy Spirit,* overlaid within and without, as it were, by *purest gold* of the word of God . . . Tell me, O Blessed Mary, what it was that was conceived by you in the womb; what it was that was borne by you in a Virgin's womb. It was the Word of God, firstborn from Heaven. (Hippolytus of Rome, *Discourse on Psalm 23* [2nd–3rd century A.D.])[34]

O noble Virgin, truly you are greater than any other greatness. *For who is your equal in greatness, O dwelling place of God the Word?... O [Ark of the New] Covenant, clothed with purity instead of gold! You are the Ark in which is found the golden vessel containing the true manna, that is, the flesh in which divinity resides...* You carry within you the feet, the head, and the entire body of the perfect God ... you are God's place of repose. (Athanasius of Alexandria, *Homily from the Papyrus of Turin* [4th century A.D.])[35]

The Mother, Virgin and blessed, was even more beautiful than the Ark full of mysteries of the house of God ... While the Ark was being carried, David had danced for joy ... *He typified in figure the way of Mary with John [the Baptist], for also that maiden was the Ark of the Godhead.* (Jacob of Serug, *Homily III on the Mother of God,* 671 [5th–6th century A.D.])[36]

Notice how these ancient Christians get their beliefs from the Old Testament, and not just the New Testament. Notice also that they base their beliefs about Mary on what they believe about Christ. Nor has this ancient belief disappeared. It continues to be taught in the recent *Catechism of the Catholic Church,* which states: "Mary, in whom the Lord himself has just made his dwelling, is ... the ark of the covenant" (CCC 2676).

The Assumption of Mary into Heaven

As we will see in Chapter 4, the New Testament depicts Jesus as a new Davidic king—a kind of "new David" (cf. Matthew 1:1). Now, if Mary is the new Ark of the Covenant, then it makes sense that Jesus, the new David, would bring her up into heaven to be with him forever in the heavenly Temple. In other words, the New Testament revelation of Mary as the new Ark is essential for understanding the belief in her bodily assumption into heaven.[37]

In order to see this clearly, it's important to recall that once David was made king, one of his first priorities was to "bring up" the Ark to Jerusalem and place it "inside" the Tabernacle (2 Samuel 6:17). As we saw earlier, this momentous event was memorialized in Psalm 132: "Arise, O LORD, and go to your resting place, you and the ark of your might" (Psalm 132:8). Now, if Jesus is the new David, who has ascended into the heavenly Jerusalem, then it makes sense that he would likewise bring the true Ark of the Covenant—his mother—into the heavenly Temple.

That, at least, is what ancient Christians believed. To be sure, the earliest references to Mary being "taken up" into heaven that we possess base their claim on the fact that the "woman" in Revelation 12 is "in heaven."[38] However, later Christian writers linked it with her identity as the Ark. Consider the beautiful words of Modestus of Jerusalem and John Damascene regarding Mary's "Dormition" or "Falling Asleep" (Greek *koimēsis*):

When she [Mary] had completed her life's voyage happily . . . the one who gave the Law on Sinai, and who administered it from Sion, *our God, summoned his ark of sanctification to be brought home from Zion to himself, just as David, her ancestor, had said of her in a psalm, "Go up, O Lord, to the place of your rest, you and your ark of sanctification"* (Ps 132:8). She is not carried like Moses' ark of old, drawn by oxen, but she is escorted and surrounded by an army, heaven's holy angels (Modestus of Jerusalem, *Encomium on the Dormition of Mary*, 4 [7th century A.D.])[39]

Today the holy, incomparable virgin enters the heavenly sanctuary that lies above the universe . . . *Today the holy, living ark of the living God*, the one who carried her own maker within herself, *comes to her rest in the temple of the Lord not made by hands. David—her ancestor and God's—leaps for joy*; the angels join in the dance. (John Damascene, *On the Dormition of Mary*, II.2 [8th century A.D.])[40]

In light of such words, it comes as no surprise that when Pope Pius XII eventually defined the dogma of Mary's bodily assumption into heaven, in 1950, he specifically cited Modestus of Jerusalem and John Damascene as examples of ancient Christian writers who "looked upon the Ark of the Covenant, built of *incorruptible wood* and placed in the Lord's temple, as *a type of the most pure body of the Virgin Mary*, preserved and exempt from all the corruption of the tomb and raised up to such glory in heaven" (Pope Pius XII, *Munificen-tissimus Deus*, 26).[41] For if the wood of the old Ark was both "holy" and "incorruptible," then how much more should the body of Mary, the new Ark, be not only holy but free from the corruption of the grave?

This ancient connection between the Ark, the woman, and the bodily assumption of Mary makes sense when we remember that the new Ark is not just Mary's soul but her *body*. In the recent words of Pope Benedict XVI:

> *The passage from the Book of Revelation also indicates another important aspect of Mary's reality.* As *the living Ark of the Covenant,* she has an extraordinary destiny of glory because she is so closely united to the Son whom she welcomed in faith and generated in the flesh, as to share fully in his glory in Heaven. This is what the words we have heard suggest: "A great portent appeared in heaven, a woman clothed with the sun..." (Rev 12:1)... Mary, Mother of God, full of grace, fully docile to the action of the Holy Spirit, *already lives in God's Heaven with her whole being, body and soul.*" (Benedict XVI, "Homily Mass for the Solemnity of the Assumption of the Blessed Virgin Mary," August 15, 2011)[42]

In other words, it was in Mary's body that "the Word" became "flesh" and "dwelt among us" (John 1:14). Therefore it is fitting that her body, the true Ark, be taken up into the heavenly Holy of Holies.

Mary's Assumption: A Sign of Our Resurrection

I began this chapter with the modern-day quest for the lost Ark. We can bring it to a close by returning to the question Where is the "lost" Ark? Was it taken to Babylon? Is it somewhere in Ethiopia? Is it hidden in Mount Nebo?

At the end of the day, it really doesn't matter. In fact, the book of Jeremiah actually contains a prophecy that in the future age, "the ark of the covenant . . . shall not come to mind, or be remembered, or missed; it shall not be made again" (Jeremiah 3:16). After all, the New Testament tells us exactly where the *true Ark* is: "in heaven" (Revelation 11:19). In this way, it shows us that the old Ark of the Covenant has been transcended by the true dwelling place of God: Mary, the mother of "the Word" made "flesh" (John 1:14). She is the one who, through God's grace, has been made completely holy. She is the one whose body has been preserved from corruption and taken up into the heavenly Holy of Holies to be with the risen Jesus for all eternity.

As the new Moses, Jesus ascends "into heaven" *in his body* to show us that the earthly promised land is not the ultimate destination of his "exodus" (Luke 9:31). The true exodus begins in this world and ends in the heavenly world to come. In a similar way, Mary's identity as the new Ark, who is made holy by God's grace, preserved from bodily corruption, and assumed into heaven, sheds light on the destiny of *our* bodies and souls. Jesus dies and rises again so that the body of every person can be transformed by grace into a "temple of the holy spirit" (1 Corinthians 6:19). Although Mary is just a human being, Jesus gives her a unique share in his glory. Mary's assumption shows us that bodily resurrection and ascension into heaven aren't just for Jesus. They are for us too.[43]

But the mysteries of the mother of the Messiah do not end here. We have still not answered what is perhaps the most pressing question for many: Why is so much *honor* given to Mary? Why the veneration? In order to explain this, we need to turn to the third key prefiguration of Mary in Jewish Scripture: the royal queen mother.

chapter 4

THE QUEEN MOTHER

◇◇◇◇◇

As an American, I can safely say that I have no firsthand experience of what it means to belong to a "kingdom." After all, the United States would not exist if the founding fathers had not engaged in a political revolution against the British monarchy. From a very young age, I was taught that democracy was the only sound form of government, and that monarchies were, as a rule, bad. As a result, I grew up with a kind of built-in suspicion of kings and queens, to say nothing of "empires"—kingdoms that conquer other nations. Indeed, one of the first movies I ever saw in the theater was *Star Wars*, in which the good guys are all part of "the Rebellion," and the bad guys all belong to "the Empire."

Despite my personal biases, the idea of a "kingdom"—a nation ruled by the sovereign heir of a royal family—is essential for understanding the Bible's message of salvation. Think about it for a minute. At the very center of the Old

Testament stands God's promise to King David that the "throne" of David's "kingdom" would be established "forever" (2 Samuel 7:13). In other words, God promises David an *everlasting monarchy*. Likewise, when we turn to the New Testament, Jesus himself defines the "gospel" in terms of the coming of a kingdom: "Jesus came into Galilee, preaching the gospel of God, and saying . . . *'The kingdom of God is at hand;* repent, and believe in the gospel'" (Mark 1:14–15). In other words, Jesus is saying that the time has come for the empire of God—the kingdom that will rule over all the other nations of the world.[1]

The centrality of this ancient Jewish hope for an everlasting empire of God is why the New Testament opens with a detailed (some would say too detailed!) genealogy of Jesus (see Matthew 1:1–17). The whole point of the genealogy is to show Jesus is *royalty;* he is the heir to David's throne. As the first line of the Gospel states:

> The book of the genealogy of Jesus Christ, *the son of David*, the son of Abraham. (Matthew 1:1)

Likewise, when the angel Gabriel appears to Mary, he explicitly links the birth of the child to the fulfillment of God's promise to King David:

> And the angel said to her, "Do not be afraid, Mary, for you have found favor with God. And behold, you will conceive in your womb and bear a son, and you shall call his name Jesus. He will be great, and will

be called the Son of the Most High; and *the Lord
God will give to him the throne of his father David, and
he will reign over the house of Jacob forever; and of his
kingdom there will be no end."* (Luke 1:30–33)

Taken as a whole, the New Testament clearly depicts Jesus
as the long-awaited Davidic king—also known as "the Messiah" (Greek *christos*)—who has come to inaugurate the everlasting kingdom promised by God to David. Jesus isn't just a
new Adam, or a new Moses. He is also a new David.[2]

The reason all of this matters for us can be expressed in
a simple question: *If Jesus is the new Davidic king, then who is
the new queen?* Although modern-day Bible readers might not
think of a queen when it comes to the kingdom of God, as
any first-century Jew would have known, under the reign of
David's royal family, the kingdom was ruled by both a king
and a queen. Unlike in modern-day kingdoms, however, the
queen of Israel was not the king's wife but his mother. She
was known as the "queen mother" (Hebrew *gebirah*).

In this chapter, we will explore how the New Testament
depicts Mary as the new queen mother of the kingdom of
God. Moreover, we'll see how her identity as the new *gebirah* has direct implications for Catholic and Orthodox beliefs
about Mary as "mother of God," as well as the ancient Christian practices of honoring Mary and asking for her intercession. In order to see all this clearly, however, we have to back
up quite a bit and make sure we are familiar with the role
and identity of the queen mother in the Old Testament and
ancient Jewish tradition.

THE QUEEN MOTHER IN ANCIENT ISRAEL

I think it's safe to say that of the many figures in the Jewish Bible, the "queen mother" is not one of the most familiar. One reason is that she does not appear until the books of 1 and 2 Kings, which tell the history of King David and his successors. For many readers, this part of the Bible is just not as familiar as the earlier books of Genesis and Exodus. Moreover, when the story of David and his kingdom is put into art or film, the figure of the queen mother is invariably left out. Nevertheless, during the time of the Davidic kingdom, the office of the "queen mother" was very significant. For our purposes here, four aspects of her role and identity stand out.

The Queen Is the King's Mother

As I already noted, in contrast to most kingdoms, in ancient Israel, the "queen" of the kingdom was not the king's wife but his mother.[3] Her royal title—"queen mother" (Hebrew *gebirah*)—is the feminine form of the word "master" (Hebrew *gebir*). It can also be translated "great lady" or "mistress" (see 1 Kings 15:13; 2 Chronicles 15:16; Jeremiah 29:2).[4] Indeed, in the historical books of the Old Testament, the queen mother holds a position of great honor. For example, in the genealogical introduction to each new king, it is the king's mother, not his wife, who is mentioned (e.g., 1 Kings 15:1–2).

Nowhere is this clearer than in the story of the first queen mother: Bathsheba, the wife of David and the mother of King Solomon.[5] While King David is still alive, his wife pays homage to him. For example, whenever Bathsheba comes into David's presence, she "bows" to him, "does obeisance to the king," and calls him "My lord" (Hebrew *'adoni*) (1 Kings 1:16–17). Once King David is dead, however, and Bathsheba's son Solomon sits on the royal throne, the roles are reversed.[6] Now that her son is king, it is the king who *honors his mother*—not just by rising in her presence and bowing to her but by seating her on a royal "throne":

> So Bathsheba went to King Solomon, to speak to him on behalf of Adonijah. *And the king rose to meet her, and bowed down to her;* then he sat on his throne, and *had a throne brought for the king's mother;* and *she sat on his right.* (1 Kings 2:19–20)[7]

It is hard to overestimate the significance of this passage for understanding the dignity possessed by the mother of the king. Although some English translations say that King Solomon has a "seat" brought for his mother, the actual word is "throne" (Hebrew *kisse'*; Greek *thronos*). It's the exact same word used in the previous verse to describe Solomon's "throne."[8] The obvious implication of seating his mother beside him on a throne is that she—and not his wife—is queen.

The Queen Mother Reigns with the King

Equally important, the mother of the king was not merely honored with the title of queen mother. She also held an "official position in the kingdom," second in rank only to the king himself.[9] In other words, the queen mother *reigned* alongside the king.

This royal authority of the queen mother was symbolized in two key ways. First, like the king, the queen mother wore a "crown."[10] Consider, for example, the oracle of the prophet Jeremiah against the king and his mother:

> Say to *the king* and *the queen mother*:
> "Take a lowly seat,
> for *your beautiful crown*
> has come down from your head."
> (Jeremiah 13:18)

Moreover, as we just saw in the story of King Solomon, the queen mother is seated at the "right hand" of the king (1 Kings 2:20). Something similar occurs in one of the Psalms of the "Sons of Korah," which were written after the time of David. Psalm 45 describes the queen mother as standing "at the right hand" of the king:

> *Your throne, O God, endures forever and ever.*
> *Your royal scepter is a scepter of equity;*
> you love righteousness and hate wickedness.
> Therefore God, your God, has anointed you
> with the oil of gladness above your fellows;
> your robes are all fragrant with myrrh and aloes and
>   cassia.
> From ivory palaces stringed instruments make you
>   glad;

daughters of kings are among your ladies of honor;
at your right hand stands the queen in gold of Ophir.
(Psalm 45:6–9)[11]

As Old Testament scholars agree, the "queen" (Hebrew *shegal;* Greek *basilissa*) in this Psalm is the king's mother, not one of his wives.[12] The fact that she stands at the king's "right hand" means that she has a share in his authority (Psalm 45:9), just as the king who sits at the "right hand" of God shares in God's authority (Psalm 110:1). In the words of one Old Testament expert, after "the monarch himself," the queen mother has "the place of highest honor" in the kingdom.[13]

The Queen Mother Is a Powerful Intercessor

According to the Old Testament, the queen mother was also a powerful *intercessor* with her son. This makes sense. If you want to obtain a request from the king, having his mother as your advocate is a very good idea.

Consider, for example, the story of Adonijah—one of David's younger sons—who asks Bathsheba as queen mother to intercede for him with King Solomon:

> Then Adonijah the son of Haggith came to Bathsheba the mother of Solomon. And she said, "Do you come peaceably?" He said, "Peaceably." Then he said, "I have something to say to you." She said, "Say on" . . . And he said, *"Pray ask King Solomon—he will*

> *not refuse you*—to give me Abishag the Shunammite
> as my wife." Bathsheba said, *"Very well; I will speak*
> *for you to the king."* (1 Kings 2:13–14, 17–18)

Notice here that Adonijah assumes that the queen mother will "speak to the king" on his behalf and that King Solomon "will not refuse" any request made by his mother. Unfortunately, Adonijah's strategy ultimately does not work out, since Solomon has his brother put to death. Despite Solomon's abuse of his power, the passage provides an important window into the queen mother's role as royal advocate and intercessor.[14]

The Queen Mother Appears in Prophecies of the Future

Finally, the queen mother is not just someone who belongs to Israel's past. She also appears in prophecies of the future king of Israel, later known as "the Messiah." Let's look at two examples.

First, there is the famous prophecy of the mother of "Immanuel." In the early eighth century B.C., the prophet Isaiah goes to Ahaz the king and declares that God will give him the following miraculous "sign":

> The LORD spoke to [King] Ahaz, "Ask *a sign* of
> the LORD your God; *let it be deep as Sheol or high*
> *as heaven."* But Ahaz said, "I will not ask, and I will
> not put the LORD to the test." And he said, "Hear
> then, *O house of David!* Is it too little for you to
> weary men, that you weary my God also? *Therefore*

the LORD himself will give you a sign. Behold, a
maiden shall conceive and bear a son, and shall call his
name Immanuel. (Isaiah 7:10–14)[15]

Throughout the centuries, Jewish and Christian commentators have vigorously debated the meaning of the miraculous "sign," the connotation of the unusual word "maiden"
(Hebrew *'almah*), and the identity of the child "Immanuel"
(Hebrew for "God-with-us"). Does the prophecy refer to
the natural conception and birth of King Hezekiah, during
whose life the threat of an Assyrian invasion surprisingly
ceased? Or does it refer to the miraculous conception and
birth of a future king? Unfortunately, we do not have the
space here to dive into this age-old debate.[16] For our purposes, we need only make one basic point: However one interprets the prophecy, the "maiden" is the *mother of the future
king.* As such, the mother of Immanuel would by definition
also be the "queen mother."

Second, there is the prophecy of the mother of the king
from Bethlehem (Micah 5:2–3). Here the prophet Micah
speaks of a future king who is a new David. Just as King
David was born and raised in Bethlehem, so the future
"ruler" will "come forth" from Bethlehem:

You, O Bethlehem Ephrathah, who are little to be
among the clans of Judah, *from you shall come forth*
for me one who is to be ruler in Israel, whose origin
is from of old, from ancient days. Therefore he shall
give them up until the time when *she who bears gives*
birth. (Micah 5:2–3)[17]

Notice here that although the future king comes from Bethlehem, his "origin" is actually "from ancient days" or "from days of eternity" (Hebrew *mime 'olam*) (Micah 5:3). As one contemporary scholar points out, this verse suggests that "the Ruler will be a superhuman being, associated with God from the beginning of time."[18] Notice also the mysterious figure of "she who is in travail" or, more literally, "she who gives birth" (Micah 5:3).[19] In context, this verse refers to the "human mother" of the future king and thus to the "birth of the Messiah."[20]

In fact, several Old Testament scholars have suggested that Micah's prophecy of the woman who will "give birth" to the Messiah in Bethlehem (Micah 5:2–3) is actually *based on* Isaiah's earlier prophecy of the maiden who "gives birth" to Immanuel (Isaiah 7:10–14).[21] If this is right, then the implications are enormous. For it would mean that the most ancient Hebrew interpretation of the birth of Immanuel that we possess saw Isaiah 7 as a prophecy of the Messiah, who will be born in Bethlehem.

In summary, in ancient Israel, the queen of the kingdom was the king's mother. As the "great lady" (Hebrew *gebirah*), she not only wore a royal crown and sat on a royal throne, she also reigned with the king and held an office second only to that of the king himself. Small wonder then that when the prophets began to speak of the future king, the Messiah, they also spoke of the future queen mother. In light of this, one can easily imagine Jewish women in the first century not only wondering "Who will be the mother of the long-awaited Messiah?" but "Who will be the new queen mother?"

MARY THE NEW QUEEN

With all of this biblical background in mind, we can try once again to see Mary of Nazareth through ancient Jewish eyes. When we do so, we discover that Mary is much more than just the woman who happened to give birth to Jesus. She is also the *queen mother of the Messiah's kingdom*.[22] In order to see this clearly, we need to look carefully at the descriptions of Mary found in the Gospel of Matthew, the Gospel of Luke, and the book of Revelation.

The Gospel of Matthew: The Mother of Immanuel

The first evidence for seeing Mary as the new queen of the Messiah's kingdom comes from the very first line of the New Testament: "The genealogy of Jesus Christ, the son of David" (Matthew 1:1).

As any first-century Jew would have known, if Jesus is the royal "Messiah" (Greek *christos*), then by definition, Mary, his mother, is the new queen.[23] In support of this point, notice that Matthew actually names Mary at the end of Jesus' royal genealogy:

> Jacob the father of Joseph *the husband of Mary, of whom Jesus was born, who is called Christ.* So all the generations from Abraham to David were fourteen generations, and from David to the deportation to Babylon fourteen generations, and from the deportation to Babylon to *the Christ* fourteen generations. (Matthew 1:16–17)

Although people frequently claim that Hebrew women were not usually included in ancient genealogies, this is not entirely true. As we saw before, in the Jewish Scriptures, *one kind of woman was always named* in the genealogical introductions to the reigns of the Davidic kings—the royal queen mother. In the books of Kings, almost every time a new king begins to reign, the name of his royal "mother" is given (see 1 Kings 14:21; 15:1–2, 9–10; 2 Kings 8:25–26; 12:1; 14:1–2; 15:1–2, 32–33; 18:1–2; 21:1, 19; 22:1; 23:31, 36; 24:7–8, 18).[24] In the same way, Mary, the new queen mother, is named in the genealogical introduction to the new king, Jesus.[25]

Even more significant, in Matthew's account of the virginal conception of Jesus, he explicitly identifies Joseph as a member of the royal family "of David" and Mary as the mother of "Immanuel," who was spoken of by the prophet Isaiah:

> Now the birth of Jesus Christ took place in this way. *When his mother Mary had been betrothed to Joseph, before they came together she was found to be with child of the Holy Spirit;* and her husband Joseph, being a just man and unwilling to put her to shame, resolved to send her away quietly. But as he considered this, behold, an angel of the Lord appeared to him in a dream, saying, "*Joseph, son of David,* do not fear to take Mary your wife, for that which is conceived in her is of the Holy Spirit; she will bear a son, and you shall call his name Jesus, for he will save his people from their sins." *All this took place to fulfill what the Lord had spoken by the*

prophet: "Behold, a virgin shall conceive and bear a son,
and his name shall be called Emmanuel" (which means,
God with us). When Joseph woke from sleep, he did
as the angel of the Lord commanded him; he took
his wife, *but knew her not until she had borne a son;*
and he called his name Jesus. (Matthew 1:18–23)

We will return—I promise—to the implications of this passage for Mary's perpetual virginity in the next chapter. For
now, the main point is this: Whatever contemporary commentators may think, Matthew clearly interprets Isaiah's
mysterious oracle about the mother of "Immanuel" (Isaiah
7:10–14) as a prophecy of the miraculous conception of the
Messiah by an actual "virgin" (Greek *parthenos*).[26] That is
why Matthew emphasizes that Joseph "knew her not" before
Jesus was born (Matthew 1:25).[27] In other words, there is no
possibility of Joseph having mistakenly fathered the child,
since he refrained from marital relations with Mary while
she was pregnant—even though he had already taken her to
be his "wife." As the legal wife of Joseph the "son of David"
and the mother of "Immanuel," from an ancient Jewish perspective, Mary is the *royal queen mother.* She is the mother of
"God with us" (Matthew 1:23).

The Gospel of Luke: The "Mother of My Lord"

But Matthew is not the only book of the New Testament that
highlights Mary's identity as the royal queen mother. The
same is true of the Gospel of Luke.

For one thing, as we saw earlier, in the account of the

annunciation, Gabriel addresses Mary as the mother of the *Davidic king*: the child who will sit on "the throne of his father David" and whose "kingdom" will have no end (Luke 1:32). In Luke's account of the visitation, Elizabeth even more clearly addresses Mary with a royal greeting:

> And when Elizabeth heard the greeting of Mary, the babe leaped in her womb; and Elizabeth was filled with the Holy Spirit and she exclaimed with a loud cry, "Blessed are you among women, and blessed is the fruit of your womb! *And why is this granted me, that the mother of my Lord should come to me?* For behold, when the voice of your greeting came to my ears, the babe in my womb leaped for joy. And blessed is she who believed that there would be a fulfillment of what was spoken to her from the Lord." (Luke 1:41–45)

In order to grasp the significance of Elizabeth's words, it's important to keep in mind that she was Mary's elder "cousin" (Luke 1:36). In an ancient Jewish context, it would have been unheard of for an older relative to honor a younger cousin in this way—unless of course the younger person was *royalty*. Indeed, Elizabeth's expression "the mother of my Lord" (Greek *kyrios*) (Luke 1:43) clearly echoes the biblical custom of referring to the Davidic king as "my lord" (Hebrew *'adon*; Greek *kyrios*) (2 Samuel 24:21; Psalm 110:1).[28] In light of this background, more than one scholar has concluded that Elizabeth is addressing Mary with a "royal title" rooted in "the queen mother tradition of the Old Testament."[29] Perhaps even more striking, the Jewish scholar Amy-Jill Levine suggests that Elizabeth's reference to my "Lord" (Greek *kyrios*) is in fact a "divine title."[30] If this is right, then for Luke, Mary is not just the mother of the messianic king; she is also the *mother of the divine Lord.*

In addition to Elizabeth's greeting, in Mary's own song of praise to God—which came to be known as the *Magnificat* (from the Latin word for "magnify")—she implies that she and her child have been exalted to sit upon royal "thrones." With the question of Mary's status as queen mother in mind, reread her famous words:

> *And Mary said,* "My soul magnifies the Lord,
> and my spirit rejoices in God my Savior,
> *for he has regarded the low estate of his handmaiden.*
> *For behold, henceforth all generations will call me blessed;*
> for he who is mighty has done great things for me . . .
> *He has put down the mighty from their thrones,*
> *and exalted those of low degree;*
> he has filled the hungry with good things,
> and the rich he has sent empty away. (Luke 1:46–49,
> 52–53)

Notice here that when Mary declares that God has "exalted those of low degree" (Greek *tapeinous*) (Luke 1:52), in context, she is referring first and foremost to *herself,* since she has already spoken about how God looked upon "the low estate" (Greek *tapeinōsin*) of his "handmaiden" (Luke 1:48). Mary is the personal embodiment of the poor and the lowly in Israel.[31] Notice also that when Mary says God has put down the mighty from their "thrones" (Greek *thronōn*), this is *royal* language. It is kings and queens who sit on "thrones," and when they are "put down" from their thrones, others must take their place.[32] Finally, when Mary uses the language of "all generations" calling her "blessed" (Luke 1:48), it sounds like the kind of thing said about royalty in the Jewish Bible. For example, Psalm 45 declares that the name of the king will be "celebrated in all generations" (Psalm 45:17).[33]

In short, Mary's *Magnificat* implies that, although in the eyes of the world she is just a lowly "handmaiden," both she and her son have been exalted to sit upon the "thrones" of the Davidic king and his mother.

The Book of Revelation: The Queen "in Heaven"

Last, but certainly not least, there is the evidence from the book of Revelation. Although we've already looked at the woman in Revelation 12 with reference to Eve and to the heavenly Ark, we need to go back once again and explore her royal identity:

> And a great portent appeared in heaven, *a woman* clothed with the sun, with the moon under her feet, and *on her head a crown of twelve stars;* she was with child and she cried out in her pangs of birth, *in anguish for delivery* . . . She brought forth a male child, one who is to rule all the nations with a rod of iron (Revelation 12:1–2, 5)

As I argued in Chapter 2, there are solid reasons for concluding that the "woman" in this vision symbolizes Mary, the mother of the Messiah, and the people of God.[34] With this premise in mind, the description of the woman in Revelation 12 sheds important light on Mary's identity as queen mother in three ways.

The first one is fairly obvious. The "woman" who is clothed with the sun is also wearing "a crown of twelve stars" (Revelation 12:2). Although in modern times simply winning a beauty pageant can qualify a woman for wearing a "crown," in ancient times, it was not so. A crown was one of *the* symbols of royal identity and authority. In the case of Revelation 12, this is indisputable, since the crown consists of "twelve stars"— which clearly symbolize the twelve tribes of Israel (cf. Genesis 37:9–10).[35] Seen in this light, the woman clothed with the sun is nothing less than the queen of the people of God, with her crown representing "a share in Christ's kingship."[36]

Second, the description of the woman in Revelation 12 appears to be based on Isaiah's prophecy about the mother of "Immanuel" (Isaiah 7:13–14). Consider, for example, the following parallels:

Mother of Immanuel	Woman Clothed with the Sun
1. A sign . . . in the height	1. A sign . . . in the heaven, a woman
2. The virgin will be with child	2. She was with child
3. And she will give birth to a son (Isaiah 7:13–14)	3. She gave birth to a son (Revelation 12:1–2, 5)

In light of such parallels—which are even clearer in Greek—there are good reasons to conclude that Revelation is depicting the woman clothed with the sun as the "maiden" mother of Immanuel in Isaiah 7:14.[37] If this is correct, then the implications are enormous. For one thing, it strengthens the conclusion that Revelation 12 is referring to an individual woman. After all, according to the New Testament, the only "virgin" who ever conceived and gave birth to the Messiah was Mary the mother of Jesus (Matthew 1:18–25). Moreover, it suggests that Matthew was not the only first-century writer who interpreted Isaiah's prophecy of the birth of Immanuel with reference to the Messiah and his mother. John of Patmos did too. Last, but not least, it drives home the point that the mother of Immanuel in Isaiah 7 is not just any woman but the royal queen mother.

Third and finally—and this is important—the woman clothed with the sun and wearing a crown of stars is standing *above* the moon and the stars "in heaven" (Revelation 12:1). Her location matters because it presents a strong parallel with Jesus' being "caught up" to the "throne" of God in heaven (Revelation 12:5; cf. 4:2). Just as Jesus is a *heavenly* king who reigns over a *heavenly* kingdom, so Mary, Jesus' mother, is a *heavenly queen*. According to the portrait of Jesus' mother in the book of Revelation, she can rightly be described as the *queen of the kingdom of heaven*. In the words of one Protestant expert on the book of Revelation, she is "the queen of the cosmos."[38]

In sum, when we look at the New Testament in the light of ancient Jewish beliefs about the kings and queens of Israel, we can see very clearly that the mother of Jesus is repeatedly depicted as the queen mother of the kingdom of God. With this in mind, we can now ask the question So what? What are the theological implications of this New Testament evidence?

MOTHER OF "GOD WITH US"

The New Testament portrait of Mary as the virgin mother of Immanuel and the queen mother of the kingdom of God provides us with the biblical foundations for three central but controversial ancient Christian beliefs and practices: (1) Mary's identity as "Mother of God" (Greek *Theotokos*); (2) honoring Mary and asking for her intercession; and (3) the difference between the veneration of Mary and the worship of God. Let's take a few moments to look at each of these carefully.

Mother of God

First and foremost, if Mary is in fact the queen mother of Jesus, the divine king, then she is rightly referred to as the "Mother of God." Since ancient times, Christians have given Mary the title of "God Bearer" (Greek *Theotokos*)—commonly translated into English as "Mother of God"—in order to emphasize the truth of Jesus' divinity.[39]

Consider, for example, the testimony of the famous ancient Christian writer Athanasius of Alexandria, who gives us one of the first indisputable references to Mary as "Mother of God."[40] In his treatise against the Arian heretics, who denied the full divinity of Jesus, Athanasius insists that God became man and that therefore Mary is the "God-bearer":

> It was for our sake that Christ became man, taking flesh from the Virgin Mary, Mother of God (*Theotokos*). (Athanasius, *Against the Arians* 3.29 [4th century A.D.])[41]

One reason Athanasius' testimony is so significant is that he is widely respected by Catholics, Orthodox, and Protestant Christians alike as *the* leading defender of orthodox teaching on Jesus' divinity. To this day, even Protestants appeal to the writings of Athanasius as the first church father to give us the list of twenty-seven books of the New Testament that all Christians accept as Scripture.[42]

But Athanasius was not the only Christian of his day to refer to Mary as "Mother of God." In the words of one of his contemporaries:

> If anyone does not admit that holy Mary is Mother of God (*Theotokos*), he is cut off from the Godhead. (Gregory of Nazianzen, *Letter* 101 [4th century A.D.])[43]

For ancient Christians such as Athanasius and Gregory of Nazianzen, to deny that Mary was the "Mother of God" was in effect to deny the central truth of Christianity: that God himself became fully human while remaining fully divine. Eventually, in order to respond to attacks on the divinity of Jesus, Christian bishops from around the world gathered at the Council of Ephesus in A.D. 431 and solemnly proclaimed that Christ was truly God and that Mary was therefore the "Mother of God" (*Theotokos*).[44] Indeed, the decree of the Council of Ephesus is the premier example of how ancient Christians' beliefs about *Mary* were ultimately based on what they believed about *Jesus*. From that day to this, the truth of Jesus' divinity and Mary's identity as *Theotokos* continues to be confessed by Catholics and Orthodox alike as an essential teaching of the apostolic Christian faith, precisely because it safeguards the truth of the incarnation (see CCC 466, 495).[45]

Unfortunately, many modern-day Christians misunderstand the meaning of calling Mary "Mother of God." Some think it means that Mary is somehow "equal to" or "greater than" God. Others think it implies that Mary is not fully human, or that she is the "Mother of the Trinity"! Nothing could be further from the truth. I cannot stress the point enough: The title "Mother of God" (*Theotokos*) does *not* mean—nor did it ever mean—that Mary is in any way a divine person. She is a mere human being, a creature. Furthermore, Mary is not the mother of God the Father; nor is she the mother of the Holy Spirit—much less of the entire Trinity. What *Theotokos* means is that Mary is the *mother of the divine Son who became man*. Once again, the title "Mother of God" is meant to illuminate the mystery of the incarnation.

Nevertheless, many Protestant Christians still object that the title is unbiblical. After all, the words "Mother of God" are never applied to Mary in the New Testament. Where did ancient Christians get this language? Why refer to Mary this way when the Bible itself does not? In response to these objections, I want to make two quick but important points.

Although the New Testament does not call Mary the "mother of God," Elizabeth, inspired by the Holy Spirit, does refer to Mary as "the mother of *my Lord*" (Luke 1:43). As we saw earlier, both Jewish and Christian scholars agree that, in context, Elizabeth's use of "Lord" refers to Jesus' kingship and his divine identity.[46] If this is correct, then the New Testament identification of Mary as the "mother" (Greek *mētēr*) of the "Lord" (Greek *kyrios*) provides a biblical foundation for the Church's teaching that Mary is also the "Mother of God."[47]

Next, it's important to remember that the title given to Mary at the Council of Ephesus was not *exactly* "Mother of God" but "God Bearer" (Greek *Theotokos*).[48] Far from being "unbiblical," *Theotokos* is a compound word that comes straight from the Bible. In order to see this, it's important to know a little Greek. The Greek word for "God" is *theos*, and the word "bearer" (Greek *tokos*) comes from the verb "to bear" (Greek *tiktō*). With this in mind, look closely again at the Gospel of Matthew:

> "A virgin shall conceive and *bear* (Greek *tiktō*) a son,
> and his name shall be called Emmanuel," which
> means, *God* (Greek *theos*) with us. (Matthew 1:23)

There it is, right there, on the first page of the New Testament! Mary is the virgin who will "bear" (*tiktō*) the child who is "God (*theos*) with us." In other words, Mary is the "God-bearer" (Greek *Theo-tokos*)! It is no wonder that it was ancient

Greek-speaking Christians who came up with this title for Mary. They were reading the New Testament in the original Greek—not in translation. And they were reading it in light of the Old Testament. For it is the prophet Isaiah who was the first to speak of a woman "bearing" a child named "God with us" (Isaiah 7:14). In fact, Athanasius himself explicitly connects the title "God-bearer" to Isaiah's prophecy of the mother of Immanuel.[49] In short, when we read the New Testament in light of the Old Testament, Mary is indeed the mother of "God with us."

Veneration and Intercession

Second, if Mary is the queen mother of the kingdom of God, then it is fitting for Christians to give her the honor due to the queen of Christ's kingdom. And if Mary the queen is alive "in heaven" (Revelation 12:1), then it makes sense for Christians to ask her to pray for them and intercede on their behalf with Jesus the king. In other words, the fact that Mary is the new queen mother provides the biblical foundations for the ancient Christian practice of venerating Mary and asking for her intercession.[50]

Think about it for a minute. Even modern-day secular nations give honor to their presidents, prime ministers, and other appointed leaders. If earthly kingdoms are right to bestow honor on earthly leaders, then how much more fitting is it to give honor to the heavenly king of the universe and his royal mother? Again, even in our own day, those who seek the aid of government leaders often ask the people closest to them to intercede on their behalf. How much more sense does it make for Christians to ask someone as close to Jesus as Mary was (and is) to intercede on their behalf? After all, the Bible commands us to "pray for one another" (James 5:16). Why should such prayers cease in heaven (cf. Revelation 5:8)?

This, at least, is how ancient Christians understood the practice of honoring Mary as queen and asking for her prayers. Consider the words of an anonymous ancient Christian prayer that was discovered on a fragment of papyrus in Egypt:

> We take refuge in your mercy, *Mother of God* (Greek *Theotokos*). *Do not disregard our prayers in troubling times*, but deliver us from danger, O only pure one, only blessed one. (Anonymous Christian prayer [3rd–4th century A.D.])[51]

In addition to this ancient Christian prayer to Mary as "Mother of God," we have solid evidence from the fourth and fifth centuries A.D. that Christians who believed in the divinity of Jesus also asked for Mary's intercession. For example, the Eastern church father Gregory of Nazianzen praises a Christian virgin named Justina, who in the face of danger, "took refuge in God" and spent time "imploring the Virgin Mary to bring her assistance, since she too was a virgin and in danger" (Gregory of Nazianzen, *Sermon* 24.9–11).[52] Perhaps even more striking, the ancient Christian historian Sozomen tells us that in the church at Constantinople, "the power of God" was demonstrated by the healing of "many diseases," and that "the power was accredited to Mary, the

Mother of God, the holy virgin, for she does manifest herself in this way" (Sozomen, *Ecclesiastical History* 7.5.3).[53]

Notice the direct link in these examples between belief in the divinity of Jesus, Mary's identity as "Mother of God," and asking for her intercession. It is precisely because she is both the mother of Jesus and the queen of the kingdom that it makes sense to honor her and to ask for her prayers. In the words of one influential Eastern Christian writer:

> Must there not therefore be a Mother of God who bore God incarnate? Assuredly she who played the part of the Creator's servant and mother is in all strictness and truth in reality *God's Mother* and *Lady* and *Queen over all created things.* (John Damascene, *On the Orthodox Faith*, 4.14 [8th century A.D.])[54]

> Neither the human tongue nor the mind of the angels that live beyond this universe can give worthy praise to her, through whom it has been granted us to gaze clearly on the glory of the Lord . . . *Let us, in holy reverence, with trembling hand and yearning soul, pay gratefully the humble first-fruits of our minds, as we must, to the Queen Mother,* the benefactress of all nature! (John Damascene, *Homily on the Dormition 1*, no. 2 [8th century A.D.])[55]

Notice here that the title "Our Lady" comes from the Greek word for a royal "Lady" (Greek *kyria*), the "Queen" (Greek *despozousa*). Thus, Mary is "Our Lady," the "Queen over all created things," because Jesus actually *is* king of the universe—not because ancient Christians sold out to paganism. In point of fact, there was no need for ancient Christians to borrow the idea of a queen from paganism, since they had already gotten it from Judaism.

Once again, this ancient Christian belief in Mary's queenship is very much alive today. In 1950, when Pope Pius XII defined the dogma of Mary's bodily assumption into heaven, he declared that she had been *"exalted by the Lord as Queen over all things,* so that she might be the more fully conformed to her Son, the Lord of lords" (CCC 966).[56] From ancient times to the present, the veneration of Mary and the custom of asking for her intercession have flowed directly from her identity as the heavenly queen of the kingdom of Christ.

Honoring Mary Versus Worshiping God

Third and finally, ancient Christians who honored Mary and asked for her intercession did not "worship" her as if she were God. In fact, the very same Christians who honored her with the title "Mother of God" also *completely rejected the idea of worshiping Mary as blasphemy and idolatry.*[57]

The clearest example of this comes from the ancient Christian writer Epiphanius of Salamis. At the end of his massive book against heresies, Epiphanius condemns one ancient sect for worshiping Mary as if she were divine.[58] He refers to this group as the *Collyridians,* because they worshiped Mary by offering a sacrificial "loaf" (Greek *kollyra*) of eucharistic bread to her.[59] Here are Epiphanius' own words:

They say that certain Thracian women there in Arabia... bake a loaf in the name of the Ever-virgin [Mary], gather together, and both attempt an excess and undertake a forbidden, blasphemous act in the holy Virgin's name, and offer sacrifice in her name with woman officiants. This is entirely impious, unlawful, and different from the Holy Spirit's message, and is thus pure devil's work, and the doctrine of an unclean spirit... *Mary should be honored, but the Father, the Son and the Holy Spirit should be worshiped; no one should worship Mary.* There is no commandment to offer the Eucharist even to a man, as though to God, let alone to a woman; not even angels are allowed such glory... Such women should be silenced by Jeremiah, and not frighten the world. They must not say, "We honor the queen of heaven (Jeremiah 51:18)"... *Mary is to be held in honor, but the Lord is to be worshiped!* (Epiphanius, *Panarion* 78.23, 4; 79.7, 5; 8, 3; 9, 4 [4th century A.D.])[60]

Notice here that Epiphanius not only condemns the "worship" (Greek *proskyneō*) of Mary by the Collyridians as heresy and idolatry. He even uses the prophet Jeremiah's passage about the "Queen of Heaven"—the same passage used by my wife's Baptist pastor all those years ago—to describe what they're doing! At the very same time, Epiphanius is equally insistent that Mary *should* be held "in honor" (Greek *timē*).

What is the difference between "honor" and "worship"? In context, the answer is clear: *the offering of sacrifice.* In both ancient Judaism and ancient Christianity—in fact, in most ancient religions—the essence of worship was sacrifice. To be sure, showing signs of honor (such as kneeling or prostration), asking for help or intercession (in prayer), and praising (usually through songs) were standard parts of worship. However, you could do any of those things— honor, beseech, praise—to human beings as well. (Think here of the honors given to a human king.) The one action that was reserved for God—and God alone—was the offering of sacrifice. For Epiphanius, therefore, the Collyridians were committing idolatry by offering the sacrificial bread of the Eucharist to Mary.

With that said, I must insist here in the strongest possible terms that this is precisely what Catholics and Orthodox Christians *do not do*. They do not offer sacrifice to Mary; they do not offer the Eucharist to her. This is the fundamental difference between the Christian veneration of Mary and the Christian adoration of God. In the words of the *Catechism of the Catholic Church*:

> The Church rightly honors (Latin *honoratur*) "the Blessed Virgin with special devotion. From the most ancient times the Blessed Virgin has been honored with the title of 'Mother of God,' to whose protection the faithful fly in all their dangers and needs ... *This very special devotion ... differs essentially from the adoration* (Latin *adorationis*) *which is given to the incarnate Word and equally to the Father and the Holy Spirit,* and greatly fosters this adoration." (CCC 971)[61]

In my opinion, the failure to distinguish between the honoring of a human being (which can involve signs of reverence and even songs of praise) and the adoration of God (which involves the offering of sacrifice) is one of the main reasons Protestants so often equate Catholic veneration of Mary with idolatry. In traditional Protestantism, worship is largely centered on doxology: prayer and songs of praise.[62] There is no ministerial priesthood, and therefore no offering of sacrifice. For Catholics and Orthodox Christians, however, worship consists above all in the offering of the Eucharist.[63] And the Eucharist is always offered to *God alone*. Since ancient times, Christians have recognized the fundamental difference between the devotion given to Mary and the adoration given to God. Christians have long honored her as the royal queen "Mother of God," but they do not worship her as God.[64]

With this in mind, we can turn at last to yet another controversial belief: the idea that Mary not only conceived Jesus while a virgin but also remained a virgin for the rest of her life.

chapter 5

THE PERPETUAL VIRGIN

◇◇◇◇◇

I will never forget the academic year 2003–4. It was my first year teaching as a full-time professor. After years of studying to earn my Ph.D., I was thrilled to finally get in the classroom and share what I'd learned. It also happened to be the year that the number one bestselling novel *The Da Vinci Code* was published. In it, the author Dan Brown claims that Jesus of Nazareth—contrary to what Christians have always believed—was married to Mary Magdalene, one of his female followers.

Lots of controversy swirled around the novel, but it was the claim that Jesus was not celibate that was at the storm center. For about a year, it felt like everyone was talking about it. The primary result for me was that I spent most of my first year as a professional academic answering questions about a pulp-fiction thriller! Over and over again—in the classroom, in the hallway, and even on airplanes—as soon as people realized I was a Bible professor they wanted to know only one thing: "What do you think about *The Da Vinci Code?* . . . Is it true?" Invariably, what they meant was "Do you really think Jesus was married?"

This is not the place to debunk the claims behind *The Da Vinci Code.* That's been done before.[1] For our purposes, the more intriguing question is Why were so many people so interested in Jesus' virginity? Why does it matter whether this particular first-century Jewish man was celibate? Two answers come to mind.

For one thing, the claim that Jesus was married calls into question the historical truth of the biblical testimony. According to the New Testament, Jesus not only lived a life of celibacy himself but also called certain of his disciples to live lives of sexual abstinence "for the sake of the kingdom of heaven" (see Matthew 19:12).[2] Moreover, the idea that Jesus was married somehow makes him more "this-worldly." As Jesus himself says in the Gospel:

> The sons of this age marry and are given in marriage; but *those who are accounted worthy to attain to that age and to the resurrection from the dead neither marry nor are given in marriage.* (Luke 20:34–35)

In other words, according to Jesus, in the final resurrection of the dead and the new creation, *everyone will be celibate.* Thus, disciples of Jesus who embrace a life of virginity now not only consecrate their bodies to God, they also begin to live out the future life of the resurrection *in the present.* Whereas married life and procreation belong to this world, in which, because of the reality of death, human beings must reproduce, the life of virginity points us to the world to come, in which death will be no more.

What does any of this have to do with Mary? Well, since ancient times, Christians have not just made bold claims about the virginity of Jesus. They have also made some striking claims about the virginity of Mary. Indeed, for almost two thousand years, Christians have claimed not only that Mary conceived Jesus while she was a virgin but that she *remained a virgin* her whole life long.

Why would ancient Christians make such a claim? Where did the idea of Mary's perpetual virginity come from? After all, doesn't the New Testament itself mention that Jesus had "brothers" and "sisters" (Mark 6:3)? Moreover, it's one thing to believe that Jesus, who had no wife, lived a virginal life. It's quite another thing to claim that Mary remained a virgin *while she was married* to Joseph.

In this chapter, we will explore the Jewish roots of Mary's perpetual virginity. As we will see, at first glance it seems as if Mary lived an ordinary married life and had other children. Upon closer inspection, however, things are not quite so clear. In fact, if we interpret the Gospel testimony in its first-century Jewish context, there are multiple lines of evidence that from the very beginning of her marriage, Mary intended to remain a virgin and that she had no other children but Jesus. We'll begin with the evidence for Mary's Jewish vow of virginity.

MARY'S JEWISH VOW

There are three frequently overlooked pieces of evidence that suggest Mary intended to remain a virgin throughout her life: (1) the vow of virginity implicit in her response to the angel Gabriel—"How shall this be, since I do not know man?" (Luke 1:34); (2) the biblical laws for vows of abstinence for married women (Numbers 30:13–16); and (3) the evidence for the unusual abstinence of Joseph and Mary on their wedding night and during her pregnancy (Matthew 1:25). In this section, we will take a few moments to look at each of these.

Mary's Response to Gabriel: An Implicit Vow of Virginity

The first important evidence that Mary intends to remain a virgin while married comes from Luke's account of the annunciation and Mary's puzzling response to the angel Gabriel. Although we've looked at this passage before, it will be helpful to reread it with the question of Mary's perpetual virginity in mind:

> In the sixth month the angel Gabriel was sent from God to a city of Galilee named Nazareth, to *a virgin betrothed to a man* whose name was Joseph, of the house of David; and *the virgin's name was Mary.* And he came to her and said, "Hail, full of grace, the Lord is with you!" But she was greatly troubled at the saying, and considered in her mind what sort of

JESUS *and the* JEWISH ROOTS *of* MARY

greeting this might be. And the angel said to her, "Do not be afraid, Mary, for you have found favor with God. *And behold, you will conceive in your womb and bear a son, and you shall call his name Jesus.* He will be great, and will be called the Son of the Most High; and the Lord God will give to him the throne of his father David, and he will reign over the house of Jacob forever; and of his kingdom there will be no end." *And Mary said to the angel, "How shall this be, since I do not know man?"* (Luke 1:26–34)[3]

For our investigation, several features of the annunciation need to be underscored.[4]

First, it is crucial to realize that Mary is *already "betrothed"* to Joseph when the angel Gabriel appears to her (Luke 1:27). According to the Jewish Scriptures, a betrothed woman was legally married. For this reason, relations between her and another man were considered adultery (Deuteronomy 22:25–27). During the period of betrothal, she and her husband would live apart for a time. At the end of the betrothal period, which sometimes lasted up to a year, the husband would bring his wife into his home during a weeklong wedding celebration and they would consummate the marriage.[5] Although it is very popular nowadays for preachers to say that Mary was an "unwed mother" when she conceived Jesus, this is just not true. At the time of the annunciation, Mary is a *married woman* who has not yet consummated her marriage with her husband.[6]

Moreover, notice that the angel Gabriel *does not say* that Mary has *already* conceived a child or that it will happen immediately. All he says is that she "will conceive" and "bear a son" at some point in the future (Luke 1:31). Once we realize that Mary is already legally married, the first part of her question to Gabriel—"How shall this be . . . ?"—appears to *make no sense*. In the words of the atheist scholar Gerd Lüdemann:

> Mary's question is hard to reconcile with v. 27: a fiancée can hardly be surprised at the promise of a child even if she has as yet had no sexual intercourse with her fiancé.[7]

Along similar lines, the famous Protestant scholar Rudolf Bultmann once admitted that "Mary's question" is "an absurd one for a bride."[8] Put yourself in Mary's place and you'll see why. If *you* were engaged to be married and an angel appeared to you and told you that you were going to have a child, would you ask, "How shall this be"? No. You would assume that you were going to conceive the child after the marriage was consummated. But this is precisely what Mary does *not* do.

So how do we make sense of Mary's question? We pay attention to the second half of her response to Gabriel, which gives the reason for her question: "How shall this be, *since I do not know man?*" (Luke 1:34). Unfortunately, some English versions mistranslate this verse with the words "since I am a virgin" (NIV) or, even worse, "since I have no husband" (RSV). This translation is downright false, since Mary does have a husband! The original Greek, however, is quite clear: "since I do not know man (*epei andra ou ginōskō*)" (Luke 1:34;

see, e.g., KJV, NRSV translation note). In the Jewish Bible, the expression "to know" is commonly used as a euphemism for marital relations, as when "Adam *knew* his wife Eve" (Genesis 4:1). Hence, Mary's words mean "I do not have sexual relations with a man."[9] They have the same force as the English words "I do not smoke." Just as someone who says "I do not smoke" means "I do not smoke (presently), nor do I have any intentions of smoking (in the future)," so Mary's words mean "I do not have sexual relations (presently), nor do I intend to have relations (in the future)."[10]

Now, this is indeed an "absurd" thing for a betrothed Jewish woman to say, especially when we recall that she was already legally married. What are we to make of Mary's response to Gabriel? In context, the best explanation is that she has taken some kind of *vow of virginity* and that she intends to remain a virgin. Consider the words of the Greek expert J. Gresham Machen (a Protestant):

> This solution [of a vow of virginity] certainly removes in the fullest possible way the difficulty . . . No objection to it can be raised from a linguistic point of view; there seems to be no reason why the present indicative, "I know," could not be taken as designating *a fixed principle of Mary's life that would apply to the future as well as to the present.*[11]

Once her intention to remain a virgin becomes clear, Mary's response to Gabriel is no longer "absurd." Instead, it makes perfect sense. In contrast to Zechariah, who doubts Gabriel's promise of Elizabeth's miraculous conception, Mary does not doubt. She simply asks the question of *how* she is going to conceive since she is a virgin and intends to remain a virgin. That is why it is only *after* Mary declares that she does not "know man" (Luke 1:34) that Gabriel responds to her question by explaining that the conception of the child will be virginal. She will conceive through the power of "the Holy Spirit" (Luke 1:35).

Of course, this explanation of Mary's response to Gabriel might make sense of Luke's text. But it faces one obvious objection: Why would a young woman who intended to remain a virgin even enter into a marriage? Is there any evidence for ancient Jewish women practicing sexual abstinence *within* the bonds of matrimony?

Unfortunately, most scholars simply assume that a vow of sexual abstinence within marriage is impossible. Indeed, they frequently claim that there is no historical evidence for the practice of sexual abstinence within marriage in ancient Judaism.[12] As a result, many modern interpreters are forced to conclude either that Mary's response is simply "absurd" or that her words are merely a "literary device" used to prompt Gabriel to say something about the virginal conception.[13]

The problem with these approaches is that they totally fail to explain the text as we have it. They also fail to take into account the fact that we *do* have evidence for vows of sexual abstinence being taken by ancient Jewish women— including *married* Jewish women. Amazingly, the evidence for vows of abstinence is not hidden in some obscure Dead Sea Scroll or extrabiblical Jewish writing. Instead, it comes straight from one of the first five books of the Bible: the book of Numbers.

The Book of Numbers: Vows of Abstinence for Married Women

Significantly, the Jewish Bible contains an *entire chapter* dedicated to *vows of abstinence* made by ancient Israelite women (Numbers 30). Unfortunately, this chapter is universally ignored by scholars who dismiss the possibility that Mary could have taken a vow of sexual abstinence. Nevertheless, it provides us with biblical evidence for vows of abstinence being taken by unmarried women, married women, and widowed or divorced women. For the sake of space, we will focus on the verses that deal with vows taken by married women:

> *If she is married to a husband, while under her vows* or any thoughtless utterance of her lips by which she has bound herself, *and her husband hears of it, and says nothing to her on the day that he hears; then her vows shall stand, and her pledges by which she has bound herself shall stand.* But if, on the day that her husband comes to hear of it, he expresses disapproval, then he shall make void her vow which was on her, and the thoughtless utterance of her lips, by which she bound herself; and the LORD will forgive her . . . *Any vow and any binding oath to afflict herself, her husband may establish, or her husband may make void.* But if her husband says nothing to her from day to day, then he establishes all her vows, or all her pledges, that are upon her; he has established them, because he said nothing to her on the day that he heard of them. *But if he makes them null*

*and void after he has heard of them, then he shall bear
her iniquity.* These are the statutes which the LORD
commanded Moses, as between a man and his wife.
(Numbers 30:6–8, 13–16)

Several features of this biblical statute stand out as important.

First, notice that the law revolves around a woman's vow
to "afflict herself" or as the NRSV translates it, to "deny herself" (Hebrew *'annoth naphesh*) (Numbers 30:13). Although
this Hebrew expression is often used to refer to fasting, it
also includes *abstinence from sexual relations.*[14] For example,
the book of Leviticus uses the same expression to describe
fasting and abstinence from marital relations on the Day
of Atonement. On that day, Moses says to the people, "You
shall deny yourselves" (Leviticus 16:29 NRSV). Indeed, as
the contemporary Jewish scholar Jacob Milgrom points out,
the most ancient interpretations of this verse that we possess
understand the idea of self-denial or self-affliction to include
abstinence from "marital intercourse" (Mishnah, *Yoma* 8:1).[15]

Second, once the meaning of a woman "denying herself"
is linked to sexual abstinence (Numbers 30:13), the whole
chapter on women's vows makes sense. In essence, it envi-
sions vows of abstinence taken by three categories of women:
(1) unmarried women (Numbers 30:3–5); (2) married women
(Numbers 30:6–8, 13–15); and (3) widowed or divorced
women (Numbers 30:9–12). In all three cases, the binding
nature of the woman's vow is dependent on whether her father or her husband, upon hearing of the vow, says nothing
against it and thereby consents to it.

Third—and this is significant—if the father or husband

hears of the woman's vow and accepts it, then the vow is *perpetually binding.* Although the teaching in Numbers 30 could conceivably be applied to temporary vows, the context suggests the primary meaning is permanent vows. After all, what meaning would a temporary vow of sexual abstinence have for an unmarried virgin in her father's house? The text makes sense only if it refers to a permanent vow of abstinence, of which the girl's father approves. Likewise, what meaning would a temporary vow of abstinence have for a widow? If she had taken a vow of temporary abstinence from relations with her husband, she would (obviously) be automatically released from the vow by his death! (Think here of the prophetess Anna, whose husband died only "seven years" after their marriage but who chose to remain "a widow" praying and fasting in the Temple until she was eighty-four [Luke 2:36–37].) If a permanent vow of sexual abstinence is in view in both of these cases, then it makes sense to suggest a *permanent* vow of sexual abstinence for a married woman is also in view.

This at least would explain why the law specifically mentions a husband's right to "make void" his wife's vow to "deny herself" (Numbers 30:13). Now, it is possible that ancient Israelite husbands were so fed up with their wives' constant fasting that a law had to be created to deal with it. But I find it much more likely that women's vows of sexual abstinence led to laws being enacted to regulate the practice of abstinence from sexual relations. Indeed, it is very easy to imagine a situation in which the husband might later change his mind and decide to make his wife's vow to deny herself "null and void" (Numbers 30:15).

Finally, it is important to point out that later Jewish writings outside the Bible confirm the biblical evidence for various kinds of women taking vows of sexual abstinence.[16] For example, the first-century Jewish historian Josephus tells us that some married Jewish men and women who belonged to the sect of the Essenes would voluntarily abstain from relations for up to "three years" at a time (Josephus, *War* 2.160–61). Likewise, the first-century Jewish writer Philo of Alexandria describes another Jewish sect, known as the Therapeutae, which consisted of both celibate Jewish men and "aged virgins (Greek *parthenoi*), who have kept their chastity not under compulsion, like some of the Greek priestesses, but of their own free will" (Philo, *On the Contemplative Life*, 68). Last, but not least, it is worth noting that the ancient collection of Jewish traditions known as the Mishnah (usually dated around 200 A.D.) contains explicit references to married Jewish men and women taking "vows" to abstain from ordinary marital relations. If such vows became too extreme, they could be grounds for divorce (see Mishnah, *Ketuboth* 7:3–7; *Nedarim* 11:1–12).[17]

What is the upshot of this ancient Jewish evidence? Simple: If a young Jewish woman—say, Mary—takes a vow to "deny herself" (Numbers 30:13), and her legal husband—in our case, Joseph—hears of the vow *and says nothing*, then the vow stands, and she is bound by the Torah to keep it. In other words, it is the Bible itself that provides a solid historical basis for Joseph and Mary practicing sexual abstinence within marriage. Indeed, the book of Numbers is very explicit that if the husband changes his mind "and makes them [the vows] null and void after he has heard of them," then *the sin will be upon him*: "he shall bear her iniquity" (Numbers 30:15). But as Matthew's Gospel tells us: Joseph was a "righteous man" (Matthew 1:19); he was obedient to the Law. If Mary took a vow of sexual abstinence—and her words "How can this be, since I do not know man?" (Luke 1:34) constitute evidence that she did—and if Joseph accepted this vow at the time of their betrothal, then he would have been bound by Mosaic Law to honor her vow of sexual abstinence under the penalty of sin.

The Evidence for Joseph's Abstinence

In case there is any doubt about all this, we need to turn to the third piece of evidence for Mary having taken a vow to refrain from ordinary marital relations. I'm speaking of the Gospel of Matthew's account of Joseph's abstinence:

> Behold, an angel of the Lord appeared to him in a dream, saying, *"Joseph, son of David, do not fear to take Mary your wife*, for that which is conceived in her is of the Holy Spirit; she will bear a son, and you shall call his name Jesus, for he will save his people from their sins" . . . When Joseph woke from sleep, he did as the angel of the Lord commanded him; *he took his wife, but knew her not until she had borne a son*; and he called his name Jesus. (Matthew 1:20–21, 24–25)

To be sure, this passage is one of the most frequently cited proofs against the perpetual virginity of Mary. However, if we interpret it in its first-century Jewish context, it actually provides important corroboration *for* the evidence in Luke's Gospel that Joseph and Mary do not engage in ordinary marital relations.

To begin with, although at first glance the statement that Joseph did not "know" Mary "until (Greek *heōs*) she bore a son" (Matthew 1:25) may seem to imply that Joseph did have relations with Mary after the birth, this is actually not the case. The Greek word "until" (*heōs*) simply describes a certain period of time, and does not imply anything about what happens afterward. Consider, for example, the following examples from Matthew's Gospel, in which the word "until" (Greek *heōs*) clearly does *not* imply a change afterward:

> "The Lord said to my Lord, 'Sit at my right hand, *until* (Greek *heōs*) I put your enemies under your feet.'" (Matthew 22:44)

> Jesus came and said to them . . . "Lo, I am with you always, *until* (Greek *heōs*) the end of the age." (Matthew 28:20)

Perhaps the most striking example of all comes from the account in the Greek Old Testament of what happened to King David and his wife Michal after she despised him for dancing:

> And Michal the daughter of Saul had no child *until* (Greek *heōs*) the day of her death. (2 Samuel 6:23 LXX)[18]

Obviously, the use of "until" here doesn't imply that Michal began having children after she died! In light of such linguistic parallels, both Protestant and Catholic scholars agree that Matthew's use of the word "until" (*heōs*) with reference to Joseph's abstinence simply *does not imply anything* about what happened after Jesus was born.[19] One Protestant expert on Matthew's Gospel calls this fact "indisputable."[20] If this is true, then Matthew's reason for emphasizing Joseph's abstinence is not to deliver a preemptive strike against belief in the perpetual virginity of Mary. Instead, Matthew's point is to show that *there is no way Jesus was Joseph's son,* because Joseph did not have relations with Mary at any time during her pregnancy.[21]

In making this point about the virginal conception, however, Matthew reveals something extremely significant: *Unlike an ordinary Jewish couple, Joseph and Mary did not consummate their marriage on their wedding night.* Although it is easy to fly right by this point, it demands some scrutiny. From a historical perspective, how does one explain the abstinence of Joseph and Mary on their wedding night? In ancient Judaism, the climax of the wedding celebration was the consummation of the marriage on the wedding night in the "bridal chamber" (e.g., Matthew 9:15; 25:1–13). Yet Matthew clearly states that although Joseph "took" Mary to be his "wife," they did not consummate their marriage on their wedding night (Matthew 1:24–25). And why don't Joseph and Mary consummate their marriage either on their wedding night or during the pregnancy? After all, nothing in the virginal conception of Jesus would prohibit them from having ordinary marital relations.

The only plausible explanation for the abstinence of Joseph and Mary on their wedding night is that *Mary had taken a "vow" of abstinence, in accordance with Numbers 30, and Joseph had accepted it.* Indeed, taken together, the best explanation for these three pieces of evidence—Mary's declaration to Gabriel that she "knows not man" (Luke 1:34), the biblical laws for "vows" of "self-denial" taken by married women (Numbers 30:6–8, 13–16), and Joseph's willingness to abstain from ordinary relations with Mary (Matthew 1:24–25)—is that Mary of Nazareth had at some point taken a vow of abstinence, which Joseph her husband agreed to honor from the very beginning of their marriage.

Why would Joseph accept such an arrangement? We can only speculate. The Bible itself does not say. But if Joseph had even the slightest clue that Mary's body had been "overshadowed" by the "power of the Most High" (Luke 1:35)—that she was in some way like a new Ark—then you can understand why he would consider her consecrated to God. If the old Ark of the Covenant was so holy that a Levite could not even *touch* it and live (2 Samuel 6:6), then how much more the new Ark? If the earthly Temple in Jerusalem was so holy that even the priests were required to refrain from sexual relations before entering it (Exodus 19:15; 1 Samuel 21:4), then how much more Mary's body, the new dwelling place of God?[22]

In any case, at this point, I can easily imagine a reader objecting: But what about the brothers of Jesus? Don't the Gospels explicitly say that Mary had other children?[23] To that question we now turn.

THE BROTHERS OF JESUS

As is well known, the New Testament contains several references to the "brothers" and "sisters" of Jesus.[24] At first glance, these passages seem to be the strongest argument against Mary's perpetual virginity. They are certainly the most popular reason for thinking Mary had other children besides Jesus. Once again, however, we need to examine this evidence in its ancient Jewish context. When we do so, some of the very passages that mention Jesus' "brothers" actually present important evidence that Mary did *not* have other children. Let's take a few moments to examine the data.[25]

The "Brothers" of Jesus = Sons of a Different Mary

The first and most important reason for concluding that the "brothers" of Jesus are not children of Mary is also the most often overlooked. It is this: *The Gospels themselves explicitly state that the so-called brothers of Jesus are in fact the children of another woman named Mary.*

In order to see this clearly, all we need to do is compare the identities of the "brothers" of Jesus in the account of Jesus' ministry in Nazareth with the accounts of the people present at his crucifixion and burial. For the sake of convenience, I will focus on the evidence in the Gospel of Mark, paying close attention to the *names* of Jesus' "brothers":

> He went away from there and came to his own
> country ... And on the Sabbath he began to teach
> in the synagogue; and many who heard him were

astonished, saying, ". . . Is not this the carpenter, the son of Mary and *brother of James and Joses and Judas and Simon, and are not his sisters here with us?"* (Mark 6:1–3)

And Jesus uttered a loud cry, and breathed his last . . . There were also women looking on from afar, among whom were Mary Magdalene, and *Mary the mother of James the younger and of Joses,* and Salome, who, when he was in Galilee, followed him, and ministered to him. (Mark 15:37, 40–41)

On the one hand, the Gospel of Mark indisputably identifies "James" and "Joses" as two of the "brothers" (Greek *adelphoi*) of Jesus (Mark 6:3). As any Greek dictionary will tell you, the most common meaning of the word "brother" is the same as in English: "a male from the same womb."[26]

On the other hand—and this is crucial—the Gospel of Mark also provides solid evidence that the same two men, *"James" and "Joses," are the sons of a different woman named Mary.* This other Mary is mentioned three times in the account of Jesus' crucifixion, burial, and resurrection. At the crucifixion, she is called "Mary the mother of James the younger and Joses" (Mark 15:40). At Jesus' burial, she is called "Mary the mother of Joses" (Mark 15:47). On the morning of the resurrection, she is called "Mary the mother of James" (Mark 16:1). Who is this woman? Obviously, Mark would never refer to the mother of Jesus as "the mother of James and Joses," or "the mother of James," or "the mother of Joses," especially when he has already referred to Mary as *Jesus'* "mother" twice in his Gospel (Mark 3:31, 32).[27] Although scholars come up with some rather desperate attempts to avoid the obvious, the only plausible explanation is that the mother of James and Joses is a different Mary, and therefore, James and Joses are not the sons of the virgin Mary.[28]

In support of this conclusion, it is important to emphasize that the same thing is true of James and Joses in the Gospel of Matthew (although Matthew uses the proper Hebrew form "Joseph" rather than "Joses"). In fact, Matthew even refers to Mary the mother of James and Joseph as "the other Mary"!

> There were also many women there, looking on from afar, who had followed Jesus from Galilee, ministering to him; among whom were Mary Magdalene, and *Mary the mother of James and Joseph,* and the mother of the sons of Zebedee . . . And Joseph [of Arimathea] took the body, and wrapped it in a clean linen shroud, and laid it in his own new tomb, which he had hewn in the rock; and he rolled a great stone to the door of the tomb, and departed. Mary Magdalene and *the other Mary* were there, sitting opposite the sepulcher. (Matthew 27:55–56, 59–61; cf. 13:55)

It is not believable that Matthew would refer to the mother of Jesus as "the other Mary." Because of this, the Protestant scholars W. D. Davies and Dale Allison admit that this evidence suggests that "the brothers of Jesus" who are named earlier in the Gospel (Matthew 13:55) "were not the sons of Jesus' mother but of another Mary."[29] I agree. But I would add that the brothers of Jesus *also* cannot be the sons of Joseph from a previous marriage, as some people suggest.[30] The reason is simple. For Joseph to be a widower, his wife has to have died. But Mary the mother of James and Joseph is obviously *still alive* at the time of the resurrection!

In fact, when Luke refers to her simply as "Mary the mother of James" (Luke 24:10), a strong case can be made that he must be referring to the famous leader of the church in Jerusalem, also known as "James the Lord's brother" (Galatians 1:19). The reason is simple. In the words of Richard Bauckham: "Normally in the early church only James the Lord's brother could be called James without risk of ambiguity" (see Acts 12:17; 15:13; 21:18; 1 Corinthians 15:7; Jude 1).[31]

This leads us to the important question *If James and Joseph are the children of another Mary, then why are they called Jesus' "brothers"?* The answer is quite simple: in an ancient Jewish context, the Greek for word "brothers" (*adelphoi*) could be used as a synonym for close relatives, such as cousins. Many examples of this usage could be given.[32] For now, consider three:

> But Jacob became angry, and quarreled with Laban [his uncle]; Jacob said to Laban, "... What have you found of all the vessels of your house? Set it here before *my brothers and your brothers*, that they may decide between us two." (Genesis 31:36–37 LXX)[33]

> The sons of Mahli [were] Eleazar and Kish. And Eleazar died, but he had no sons, only daughters.

> And *the sons of Kish, their brothers, married them.*
> (1 Chronicles 23:21–22 LXX)

> On the same day the sons and *brothers* of king
> Izates ... entreated Caesar to grant them a pledge
> of protection. For the present he kept them all in
> custody; the king's sons and *relatives* he subse-
> quently brought up in chains to Rome. (Josephus,
> *War*, 6.356–57)[34]

Notice here that it is the *context* that gives us the clue to
when the word "brothers" means "relatives" or "cousins." In
context, Jacob is clearly using "brothers" (Greek *adelphoi*)
to refer to his cousins, the sons of his uncle Laban (Genesis
31:37 LXX). Likewise, in the second passage, the "brothers"
(Greek *adelphoi*) of the daughters of Eleazar are explicitly
identified as first cousins, the sons of the girls' uncle Kish.
Last, but certainly not least, Josephus proves that a first-
century Jew could use the words "brothers" (Greek *adelphoi*)
and "relatives" (Greek *syngeneis*) as synonyms in the same
Greek text.[35]

Likewise, when it comes to the "brothers" of Jesus in the
Gospels, we have to determine the meaning of the word *in
context*. If all we had were the reference to Jesus' brothers
during his ministry in Nazareth, it would be reasonable to
assume they were his blood "brothers." However, if later in
the same Gospel two of these brothers, "James and Joses,"
are explicitly identified as the children of *another woman*
named Mary, then the obvious explanation is that the word

"brothers" is being used to refer to Jesus' "relatives."[36] If there is any doubt about this, it's important to point out that *Jesus himself actually uses the word for "cousins" or "relatives" to describe his so-called brothers and sisters.* Reread the evidence from Mark, this time paying attention to Jesus' final statement:

> "Is not this the carpenter, the son of Mary and *brother* of James and Joses and Judas and Simon, and are not his *sisters* here with us?" And they took offense at him. And Jesus said to them, "A prophet is not without honor, except in his own country, and *among his own cousins* (Greek *syngeneusin*), and in his own house." (Mark 6:3–4)[37]

The word I have translated here as "cousin" (Greek *syngeneus*) is from the same Greek root as the angel Gabriel's reference to Elizabeth as Mary's "cousin" (Greek *syngenis*) (see Luke 1:36 KJV, Douay-Rheims). What possible reason can be given for Jesus referring to his "brothers" and "sisters" as his "relatives" or "cousins"? Maybe because, according to the Gospel of Mark, they *are* his cousins.[38]

Now we could just stop here. If all we had were the evidence from the Gospels of Matthew and Mark, it would be enough to conclude that the so-called brothers of Jesus are in fact his close relatives. They are the children of another woman named Mary from Galilee. But this is not the only evidence we possess.

The Other Mary = Mary the Wife of Clopas

When it comes to the identity of the brothers of Jesus, the Gospel of John also provides an important clue to the identity of "the other Mary" who was present at the crucifixion:

> But standing by the cross of Jesus were his mother, *and his mother's sister, Mary the wife of Clopas,* and Mary Magdalene. When Jesus saw his mother, and the disciple whom he loved standing near, he said to his mother, "Woman, behold, your son!" Then he said to the disciple, "Behold, your mother!" And from that hour the disciple took her to his own home. (John 19:25–27)

This account of Jesus' death provides us three more significant insights into the relationship between Jesus, Mary, and his "brothers."

First, notice that John identifies the second woman at the cross as "his mother's *sister,* Mary" (John 19:25).[39] Although it's easy to miss the point, this verse provides important support for the word "sister" (Greek *adelphē*) being used to refer to someone other than a blood sister. It seems extremely unlikely that Mary's parents would have given both her and her sister the name Mary. However, the text makes perfect sense if John is using the word "sister" to refer to a close relative of Jesus' mother.

Second, and even more important, when John refers to this woman as "Mary the wife of Clopas" (John 19:25), he gives us an important clue to the identity of "the other Mary" referred to by Matthew and Mark. If John is referring to the same Mary that Matthew and Mark say was present at the crucifixion and burial of Jesus—Mary the mother of James and Joses—then we have further evidence that James and Joses are *not* the sons of Jesus' mother. Nor are they the sons of Joseph by a previous marriage.[40] Instead, they would be the sons of another man—a man named Clopas.[41]

Third and finally, but by no means least important, in John's account, Jesus gives his mother, Mary, to the Beloved Disciple to have as "his own" mother (John 19:26–27). I cannot stress the point enough: *If Mary would have had any other children at the time of the crucifixion, it would have been unheard of for Jesus to give his mother to one of his disciples.* In an ancient Jewish context, to fail to care for one's aging parents was a grave sin—one that Jesus himself describes as a capital offense (see Mark 7:9–13).[42] Thus, the most plausible explanation for why Jesus takes such pains in the midst of dying to make sure his mother is cared for by the Beloved Disciple is that Mary has no other children. He is her only son.

Once again, we could just stop here. If we only had the evidence of the New Testament we've just surveyed, it would be enough to confidently conclude that the so-called brothers of Jesus are in fact his close relatives, the children of Mary and Clopas, relatives of Jesus' family. However, the New Testament is not the only relevant historical evidence we possess. We also have evidence for the identity of Jesus' brothers from ancient church history—evidence that is often mysteriously ignored.

The "Brothers" of Jesus = The First Bishops of Jerusalem

According to the ancient Christian historian Hegesippus—
who was apparently the first person to write a "history" of
the Church—two of the so-called brothers of Jesus (James
and Simon) also happened to be the *first two bishops of Jerusalem.*[43] Furthermore, they were widely known to be Jesus'
"cousins"! Consider the following testimony from Hegesippus, which is quoted by Eusebius in his fourth-century history of the Church:

> The same writer [Hegesippus] also [writes] . . .
> as follows: "After *James the Just* had suffered mar-
> tyrdom for the same reason as the Lord, *Simon,
> his cousin, the son of Clopas,* was appointed bishop,
> whom they all proposed because he was *another
> cousin* (Greek *anepsion*) *of the Lord.* (Hegesippus
> [2nd century A.D.], quoted in Eusebius, *Church His-
> tory,* 4.22)[44]

> After the martyrdom of James and the conquest
> of Jerusalem which immediately followed, it is said
> that those of the apostles and disciples of the Lord
> that were still living came together from all di-
> rections with *those that were related to the Lord ac-
> cording to the flesh* (for the majority of them also
> were still alive) to take counsel as to who was wor-
> thy to succeed James. They all with one consent
> pronounced *Simon, the son of Clopas,* of whom the

Gospel also makes mention; to be worthy of the episcopal throne of that parish. *He was a cousin* (Greek *anepsion*), as they say, *of the Saviour.* For Hegesippus records that *Clopas was a brother of Joseph* (Greek *adelphon tou Iōsēph*). (Hegesippus [2nd century A.D.], quoted in Eusebius, *Church History* 3.11.1–2)[45]

Amazingly, the testimony of Hegesippus that the so-called brothers of Jesus were in fact his "cousins" (Greek *anepsioi*) is frequently just ignored by scholars who assert that Mary had other children.[46] But in the face of such historical evidence, this is unacceptable. James and Simon, two of the so-called brothers of Jesus, were not obscure figures in the early Church. In fact, they were the first two bishops of Jerusalem and some of the earliest martyrs. More important, they were *known* to be "cousins" of Jesus. Notice here that Hegesippus' identification of James and Simon as Jesus' cousins is stated simply as a matter of historical *fact*. There is no evidence that he is attempting to defend Mary's perpetual virginity. To the contrary, Hegesippus is simply reporting the history of the bishops in Jerusalem. [47]

Now, if Hegesippus is right, then the earliest historical evidence we possess jibes perfectly with the New Testament evidence we saw that the so-called brothers of Jesus—James, Joseph, Simon, and Jude—were in fact the children of *another* woman named Mary (Mark 6:1–3 15:37, 40–41; cf. Luke 24:10). It also makes perfect sense if this "other Mary" is the same woman who is called the "wife of Clopas" (John 19:25):

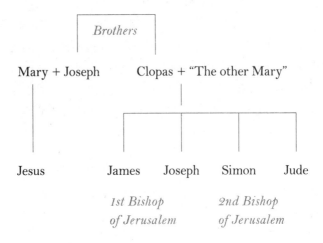

This, I would suggest, is the simplest and most histori-cally plausible solution to the mystery of the "brothers" of Jesus. Again, the best explanation for the ancient Christian claim that the "brothers" of Jesus were his cousins is that the brothers of Jesus *were actually* his cousins.[48]

EVER-VIRGIN

At this point, I suspect some readers may be surprised by what we've discovered. Maybe some of you are wondering, "Why haven't I ever heard all this before? Why didn't I know that the Gospel of Luke itself shows that Mary intended to remain a virgin? Why didn't I know that the Gospel of Mark itself shows that the so-called brothers of Jesus were children of another Mary?" I know that's what I wondered when I first stumbled onto the evidence that I've just shared with you. Whatever the reason for our lack of familiarity with this data, one thing is certain: None of it is new.

If we go back to the writings of ancient Christians out-side the New Testament, not only do we discover that they were well aware of Mary's perpetual virginity, we also learn why they thought it mattered. In this final section, we will take just a few moments to show what ancient Christians had to say about the mystery of Mary's perpetual virginity.

The Perpetual Virginity of Mary in Ancient Christianity

Nowadays, the perpetual virginity of Mary is widely rejected by Christians of many denominations, especially those who trace their origins back to the Protestant Reformation. In-deed, it has become so universally accepted that Mary had other children after Jesus that writers nowadays do not even feel they have to defend or explain the assumption that Mary had other children.

Yet it was not always so. Even a cursory study of ancient Christianity shows that from the earliest times, the belief that Mary remained a virgin was held by Christians throughout the known world.[49] Consider, for example, the following quo-tations, noting the biblical bases for their beliefs:

> *If she had had other children, the Savior would not have ignored them and entrusted his Mother to someone else* (John 19:26–27); nor would she have become someone else's mother. (Athanasius, *On Virginity* [4th century A.D.])[50]

> *The expression "until"* (Matthew 1:25) *need not lead you to believe that Joseph knew her subsequently*; rather, it is

used to inform you that the Virgin was untouched by man until the birth of Jesus. (John Chrysostom, *Homily on Matthew* 5.2 [4th century A.D.])[51]

Already before he was conceived he wished to choose for himself, in order to be born, a virgin who was consecrated to God, as is indicated by the words with which Mary responded to the angel, who was announcing her imminent motherhood: "How shall this be done, because I know not man?" (Luke 1:34). *And she certainly would not have responded in such a way if she had not already made a vow of virginity.* (Augustine, *On Holy Virginity* 4.4 [early 5th century A.D.])[52]

Notice that this testimony to Mary's perpetual virginity comes from Christians living in both the East and the West, writing in both Latin and Greek.[53] Indeed, the belief in Mary's perpetual virginity was so widespread that from early times it was regarded as a touchstone of authentic Christian teaching:

There is no child of Mary except Jesus, according to the opinion of those who think correctly about her. (Origen, *Commentary on John*, 1.4 [3rd century A.D.])[54]

Those who love Christ refuse to hear that the Mother of God ceased to be a virgin at a particular moment. (Basil of Caesarea, *Homily on the Holy Nativity of Christ*, 5 [4th century A.D.])[55]

Indeed, by the late fourth century A.D., when a Roman writer named Helvidius published a book claiming that the "brothers" and "sisters" of Jesus were the children of Mary, he brought down upon his head the wrath of the great biblical scholar Jerome. In his treatise *The Perpetual Virginity of Mary*, Jerome rooted his belief in Mary's perpetual virginity in the Bible: "We believe that God was born of a Virgin, because we read it. That Mary was married [= had sexual relations] after she brought forth, we do not believe, because we do not read it" (*Against Helvidius* 21).[56] Eventually, the belief in Mary's perpetual virginity was so universal that when Christian leaders from throughout the world gathered at the second ecumenical Council of Constantinople, in A.D. 553, they gave Mary the official title "Ever-Virgin" (Greek *Aeiparthenos*).[57]

The Perpetual Virginity of Mary: Why Does It Matter?

Of course, that still leaves us with the question So what? Why does the perpetual virginity of Mary matter? I'll offer you three closing thoughts.[58]

First and foremost, Mary's virginity matters for the same reason that the virginity of Jesus matters: because *the truth matters*. Just as it isn't right for fiction writers to claim that it is a "fact" that Jesus was married to Mary Magdalene, so it is irresponsible for scholars to ignore the evidence that Mary intended to remain, and in fact did remain, a virgin her entire life. As we have seen, Mary's perpetual virginity makes the best sense of the most evidence in the New Testament. All the other theories have gaping holes. They completely fail to explain why the same Gospels that refer to James and Joseph as the "brothers" of Jesus also identify them as the children of another woman named Mary. They also fail to explain how two of these same so-called brothers, James and Simon, went on to become the first bishops of Jerusalem and were widely known as Jesus' cousins, the sons of his uncle Clopas.

Second, the perpetual virginity of Mary matters because it points beyond her to the final resurrection of the dead and the coming of the new creation. As we saw at the beginning of the chapter, one of the reasons Jesus was celibate and called others to sexual abstinence was "for the sake of the kingdom of heaven" (Matthew 19:12), so that by their virginity, they might point to the life of "the age to come" (Luke 20:34–36)—the new world in which everyone will be celibate. Now if Mary is the new Eve of the new creation (as we saw in Chapter 2), then it makes sense that she would also choose to live out, in a unique way, the virginal life of the resurrection. *Mary's perpetual virginity thus points us to the eternal life of the world to come, the resurrection, and the new creation, in which ordinary marital relations will pass away because death will be no more.*

Finally, the perpetual virginity of Mary matters because Mary, like Jesus, is no ordinary person. As we've seen in earlier chapters, according to the New Testament, Mary is the new Eve, the new Ark, the new queen mother. As a perpetual virgin, Mary is even more than this; she also becomes a symbol of the Church, who is both the *virgin bride* of Christ and the *fruitful mother* of all Christians. In the words of Ambrose of Milan:

> Fittingly is [Mary] espoused, but Virgin because she prefigures the Church which is undefiled yet wed. A Virgin conceived us of the Spirit, a Virgin brings us forth without travail. (Ambrose, *On Luke*, 2.6–7 [4th century A.D.])[59]

Notice that last line: Mary gave birth "without travail." What does Ambrose mean?

In order to answer this question, we will need to consider the next ancient Christian belief about Mary—one that is less well known these days, but even more mysterious than her perpetual virginity. I am speaking here of the belief that not only was the conception of Jesus miraculous but *his birth was as well.* To that topic we now turn.

chapter 6

THE BIRTH OF THE MESSIAH

◇◇◇◇◇

Out of all the memorable experiences I have had in my life, the birth of my first child is right there at the top of the list. What stands out most in my memory is how the birth itself was a mysterious combination of both pain and joy.

On the one hand, I was completely taken aback by the intensity of my wife's suffering. To be sure, I had watched a video or two about what childbirth involved and had gone to all the requisite classes for husbands to learn how best to "help" their wives in the birth. Nevertheless, I was completely unprepared for the reality. Elizabeth's labor wasn't just extremely painful for her; it was extremely long, lasting some twenty-two hours. Moreover, when the time for what they called "hard labor" finally arrived, I had no idea there would be *so much blood*. I'd be lying if I didn't admit that the delivery room began to spin more than once.

On the other hand, I was equally overwhelmed by the

intensity of the joy I felt when, after all those hours, I finally saw my daughter for the first time. The sight of her jet-black hair and her tiny little face is still emblazoned in my mind. I don't need a picture to remember it. Never before in my life had I witnessed someone I love go through such agony; never before had I simultaneously tasted such overwhelming happiness. The whole birth was one giant, terrifying, tear-filled paradox.

The same thing is true of Jesus. His whole life is one great paradox—a mixture of joy and suffering. From a certain angle, much of Jesus' public ministry looks as if it is entirely devoted to taking away suffering. He heals the sick, he raises the dead, he makes the lame walk, he makes the blind see. Whether it is the woman who has bled for twelve years (Mark 5:25) or the man who has been paralyzed for thirty-eight (John 5:5), Jesus takes their pain away. Over and over again, he brings healing and joy.

Flip the coin to the other side, however, and you will see a different image: In the final analysis, Jesus' mission is not to *take away* all suffering but to *take it upon himself.* As he says to the disciples: "The Son of man did not come to be served but to serve, and to give his life as a ransom for many" (Mark 10:45). With these words, Jesus is alluding to the prophecy of the suffering Servant, who takes the pains and the sins of everyone else upon himself (see Isaiah 52:13–53:12). Likewise, in one of the last speeches he gives, Jesus warns his disciples that before "the end comes," there will be a time of suffering such as the world has never known. He even uses the image of a woman in labor to describe it: "There will be earthquakes in various places, there will be famines; *this is but the beginning of the birth-pangs"* (Mark 13:8). In short, Jesus seems to come both to take away suffering and to unleash it. Seen in this light, the miracles of Jesus are not ends in themselves. Instead, they are "signs" that point forward to the ultimate overthrow of suffering and death that will take place through his passion, death, and resurrection, and his final coming in glory.

When we turn to the figure of Mary, we find a very similar paradox. On the one hand, her life is filled with the miraculous: the appearance of the angel Gabriel, the virginal conception, the star of Bethlehem and the coming of the Magi, the dreams of Joseph, the escape from King Herod (Matthew 1–2; Luke 1–2). On the other hand, from the moment of the annunciation, Mary's life is equally full of suffering: the threat of divorce, the failure to find room in Bethlehem, the poverty of Joseph, Herod's massacre of the infants, the flight to the foreign land of Egypt, the loss of Jesus for three days in Jerusalem, and above all this, the pain of watching her son—who was also "the Son of God"—die on the cross.

In this chapter, we will discover that this mysterious combination of the miraculous and the sorrowful actually goes back to ancient Jewish prophecies about *the mother of the Messiah.* In Jewish Scripture and tradition, the Messiah's mother is paradoxically depicted both as being spared the pain of childbirth and as undergoing what came to be called the "birth pangs of the Messiah." As I hope to show, both of these prophecies are true: One points to the miraculous birth of Jesus, and the other to the mystery of his death. According to the New Testament, Mary did suffer the "birth pangs" of the cross, through which came the new life of the resurrection. This will lead to the ancient Christian belief that Mary did not suffer labor pains at Bethlehem, but she did suffer them at Calvary. In so doing, she shared in the passion of Jesus in a uniquely fruitful way.

THE MOTHER OF THE MESSIAH

In order to see clearly the Jewish roots of the Christian belief in the miraculous birth of Jesus, we will have to go back to ancient Jewish Scripture and tradition, and see what they have to say about the mother of the Messiah. When we do so, we discover two fascinating (and apparently conflicting) expectations.

Isaiah's Prophecy: The Painless Birth of the Messiah

On the one hand, the Old Testament seems to suggest that the mother of the Messiah will *not* suffer pain in childbirth. In a very important (but often ignored) prophecy, the book of Isaiah speaks of a woman who will give birth to a son without experiencing any pain:

> *Before she was in labor she gave birth;*
> *before her pain came upon her she was delivered of a son.*
> *Who has heard such a thing? Who has seen such things?*
> Shall a land be born in one day?
> Shall a nation be brought forth in one moment?
> For as soon as Zion was in labor
> she brought forth her sons. (Isaiah 66:7–8)

Notice three things about this important passage:

First, the prophecy of the painless childbirth takes place immediately after Isaiah's oracle about the coming of a new creation—"new heavens and a new earth" in which God will make a new Jerusalem (Isaiah 65:17–18). In this new creation, the effects of the sin of Adam and Eve will be undone: Men will no longer "labor in vain" and women will not "bear children for calamity" (Isaiah 65:23). In other words, two of the principal effects of the Fall—fruitless toil and pain in childbirth—will be undone (cf. Genesis 3:16–19). Second, the birth of the woman's "son" is a *miraculous* and *unprecedented* "act of the new creation."[1] It is miraculous because his mother delivers her child "before her pain came upon her" (Isaiah 66:7); it is unprecedented because nothing like this has ever happened before: "Who has heard such a thing? Who has seen such things?" (Isaiah 66:8). Third, notice that the identity of the mother in the prophecy is ambiguous.[2] At first, it appears to refer to an individual woman, who gives birth to an individual "son" (Isaiah 66:7). But then, it seems to describe the city of "Zion"—another name for Jerusalem—giving birth to multiple "children" as soon as she begins to "labor" (Isaiah 66:8).

What are we to make of this mysterious prophecy? Whatever contemporary commentators may say, for our purposes what matters is how it was interpreted in Jewish tradition. Strikingly, when we turn to ancient Jewish writings outside the Bible, the prophecy of Isaiah 66 is consistently linked with the painless birth of the Messiah. Consider the following examples:

Before distress comes to her she shall be delivered; and before shaking will come upon her, as pains upon a woman in travail, *her king will be revealed.* Who has heard of such a thing? Who has seen such things? (*Targum Isaiah* 66:7–8)[3]

The Holy One, blessed be He, was creating the light of *the Messiah*: thus . . . "Before she travailed, she brought forth" (Isa 66:7). Before the last who shall enslave [Israel] was born, *the first redeemer was born.* (*Genesis Rabbah* 85:1)[4]

In This World a woman bears children with pain, but of the Time to Come [see] what is written! "Before she will travail, she will have brought forth; before her pain will come, she will have been delivered of a man-child" (Isa 66:7). (*Leviticus Rabbah* 14:9)[5]

Notice that in the first two texts, the prophecy of Isaiah 66 is explicitly linked with the coming of "the Messiah," the future "king" of Israel. This is extremely important, for it provides evidence that at least some ancient Jews interpreted Isaiah's prophecy as a reference to the miraculous birth of the Messiah.[6] Notice also the rationale for the painless birth of the Messiah: Since pain in childbirth is a result of the sin of Adam and Eve (Genesis 3:16–19), it belongs by definition to the old creation ("this world"). In the new creation ("the world to come"), women will not experience such pain. In other words, because the Messiah himself will usher in the new creation, it is fitting that his birth would be the beginning of this new creation, in which the effects of the sin of Adam and Eve would be undone.

Micah's Prophecy: The Birth Pangs of the Messiah

With that said, the Old Testament *also* seems to suggest that the mother of the Messiah *will* suffer during her "labor." I am speaking here of the prophet Micah's famous oracle about the coming of the Messiah. Although we've looked at this passage before, let's look again, this time keeping our eyes on the imagery of labor pains:

> But you, O Bethlehem Ephrathah,
> who are little to be among the clans of Judah,
> *from you shall come forth for me*
> *one who is to be ruler in Israel,*
> whose origin is from of old, from ancient days.
> *Therefore he shall give them up until the time*
> *when she who is in labor has brought forth;*
> then the rest of his brethren shall return
> to the people of Israel. (Micah 5:2–3)[7]

Again, three aspects of this passage are worth highlighting.

First, the prophecy is clearly about the coming of the future Davidic king, the "ruler" who will come from "Bethlehem" (David's town) as well as from "ancient days." In other words, it is about the "appearance of a new Messianic king."[8] Second, the passage is also about "the human mother" of the future king.[9] She is the woman who will be "in travail" until she has "brought forth" (Micah 5:3). The Hebrew expression for being "in travail" or, more literally, "in labor" (Hebrew *yoledah*) in this verse is used elsewhere to describe the sufferings involved in giving birth to a child (Micah 4:9–10; cf. Genesis 35:16–17; Jeremiah 30:6). Third and finally, the prophecy also seems to say that the people of Israel as a whole are going to experience a time of intense suffering before the king comes: God will "give them up" until the time when "she who is in travail has brought forth" (Micah 5:3). In the Hebrew Scriptures, the prophets frequently use the imagery of a woman's "birth pangs" to symbolize the time of intense suffering that will precede the coming of the king and the resurrection of the dead (see Micah 4:9–10; Isaiah 26:16–19; Jeremiah 30:4–9). After this time of anguish, the people of Israel will "return" to the promised land, and the king himself will reign over a universal kingdom that will spread "to the ends of the earth" (Micah 5:4).[10]

What are we to make of Micah's prophecy of the woman in labor? Again, when we turn to the most ancient Jewish interpretations we possess, we discover that Micah's prophecy was linked both with the birth of the Messiah *and* with a mysterious period of tribulation known as the "birth pangs of the Messiah."[11] Consider the words of the ancient Jewish Targum and the Talmud:

> And you, O Bethlehem Ephrathah ... *from you shall come forth before me the Messiah,* to exercise dominion over Israel, he whose name was mentioned from of old, from ancient times. *Then they shall be handed over in the time when she who is in labour gives*

birth . . . He shall arise and rule with might from the Lord. (*Targum on Micah* 5:1–3)[12]

Rab said: "*The son of David* will not come until the [Roman] power enfolds Israel for nine months, as it is written: 'Therefore he will give them up, until the time that she who is in labor has brought forth: then the remnant of his brethren shall return unto the children of Israel' (Micah 5:2)." [Rabbi] Ulla said: "Let him [the Messiah] come, but let me not see him . . ." [Rabbi] Abaye inquired of Rabbah: "What is your reason? . . . *Because of the birth pangs of the Messiah?* But it has been taught, Rabbi Eleazar's disciples asked him: '*What must we do to be spared the birth pangs of the Messiah?'* " (Babylonian Talmud, *Sanhedrin* 98b)[13]

Notice once again that Micah's oracle is explicitly interpreted as a prophecy of "the Messiah." Thus, the woman who gives birth is the mother of the Messiah. On the other hand, the Talmud also interprets the sufferings of the woman as a *metaphor* for the time of tribulation that will precede the coming of the Messiah. The rabbis refer to this time of suffering as the "birth pangs of the Messiah" (Hebrew *heblo shel mashiah*) (Babylonian Talmud, *Sanhedrin* 98b). Apparently, some of them thought that the time of the Messiah would be so terrible that they were willing to miss it in order to be spared his "birth pangs." In any case, for both Jewish texts, it is only after the time of suffering that the Messiah will finally rule over his universal kingdom that reaches to the ends of the earth.

To sum up what we've learned so far: If we turn to the pages of Jewish Scripture and tradition and focus our attention on prophecies of the Messiah's birth, two apparently contrary pictures emerge. On the one hand, Isaiah prophesies that, at the time of the new creation, a woman will give birth to a son without the pain of childbirth that was part and parcel of the old creation. In later Jewish tradition, Isaiah's prophecy was interpreted as being about the birth of the Messiah. On the other hand, Micah also prophesies about the mother of the Messiah, but in this case, he says that she will suffer the pains of "labor." In later Jewish tradition, Micah's prophecy was interpreted as being about the "birth pangs" of the Messiah—a time of suffering that would precede the age of salvation.

So what are we to make of these two prophecies? What do they reveal to us about Mary, the mother of Jesus? Did she or did she not suffer the birth pangs of the Messiah? In order to answer this question, we have to turn to the writings of the New Testament, in which the mysterious image of the birth pangs of the Messiah's mother reoccurs in two key places: the book of Revelation and the Gospel of John.

MARY'S BIRTH PANGS

With these ancient Jewish prophecies and traditions in mind, we can now study the passages in the New Testament that describe Mary's birth pangs and try to see them through ancient Jewish eyes. In this case, we will begin not with the Gospel accounts but by returning once more to John's vision in the book of Revelation.

The Woman in Revelation: The "Birth Pangs" of the Crucifixion

By far the most explicit description of the birth pangs of Mary in the New Testament comes to us from John's vision of the woman clothed with the sun who gives birth to a child who is caught up into heaven (Revelation 12:1–6). As we saw in Chapter 2, there are strong arguments for concluding that "the child" who is born is primarily an individual—Jesus the Messiah—and that the woman who gives birth to the child is also primarily an individual—Mary his mother.[14] With this in mind, we can turn back to this passage one last time, this time focusing on the sufferings of the Messiah's mother:

> And a great portent appeared in heaven, *a woman clothed with the sun,* with the moon under her feet, and on her head a crown of twelve stars; *she was with child and she cried out in her pangs of birth, in anguish for delivery.* And another portent appeared in heaven; behold, a great red dragon, with seven heads and ten horns, and seven diadems upon his heads. His tail swept down a third of the stars of heaven, and cast them to the earth. *And the dragon stood before the woman who was about to bear a child, that he might devour her child when she brought it forth; she brought forth a male child,* one who is to rule all

> the nations with a rod of iron, *but her child was caught up to God and to his throne,* and the woman fled into the wilderness, where she has a place prepared by God, in which to be nourished for one thousand two hundred and sixty days. (Revelation 12:1–6)

At first glance, it seems pretty clear that if the child represents Jesus, and the woman represents Mary, then the image of her crying out "in the pangs of her birth, in anguish for delivery" (Revelation 12:2) must be a description of the painful labor she suffered at Bethlehem. Indeed, over the years, I've noticed that this is how the passage is interpreted by many of my students, who often just assume without question that Mary gave birth in an ordinary way.

As contemporary scholars have pointed out, however, this passage is not a biography but an apocalyptic vision. Indeed, there are several reasons to think that the vision of the woman in anguish for delivery is not a *literal* depiction of what Mary suffered at Bethlehem, during the birth of Jesus, but a *symbolic* depiction of *what Mary suffered at Calvary*, during the crucifixion of Jesus.[15]

For one thing, the word used to describe the "anguish" or "torment" (Greek *basanizō*) of the Messiah's mother is not normally used to describe the ordinary birth pains of a woman in labor (Revelation 12:2). As one New Testament scholar writes: "It is a fact that in the LXX [the Greek Old Testament], the New Testament, the Apocrypha, the papyri and the writings of the Fathers, there is not a single case in which the verb *basanizō* is used to refer to the pains of childbirth."[16] In the book of Revelation, the word is used to refer to "torment" or "torture" (Revelation 11:10, 9:5, 14:10, 20:10). The use of such an unusual term to describe the sufferings of the mother of the Messiah strongly suggests that Revelation is employing the language of symbolism. The imagery of birth pangs is being utilized to refer to "the tribulations at the end of the age."[17]

Even more important, if we interpret the birth of the child as a literal description of what happened at Bethlehem, we find ourselves with a problem, since immediately after the "birth," the child is "caught up to God and to his throne" in heaven (Revelation 12:5)! Where is the account of Jesus' childhood and public ministry? They are absent, because this is not a literal description of the birth of Jesus. It is a symbolic description of Jesus' death, resurrection, and ascension into heaven and his being seated at the right hand of God the Father.[18]

Finally, as both Protestant and Catholic commentators have pointed out, John's description of the woman in anguish is directly based on Isaiah's prophecy of the *painless* birth of the Messiah![19] Compare the following Greek parallels:

Mother of Messiah	Woman in Heaven
1. She who was in labor (*ōdinousan*)	1. She was in labor (*ōdinousa*)
2. She escaped (*exephygen*)	2. She escaped (*ephygen*)
3. She gave birth to a male (*eteken arsen*) (Isaiah 66:7 LXX)[20]	3. And she bore a male son (*eteken huion arsen*) (Revelation 12:2, 6, 5)

Now, if John wanted to emphasize that Mary suffered literal birth pangs, why would he allude to an Old Testament prophecy in which the mother of the Messiah escapes the pain of childbirth? I have a suggestion: because John is not interested in making sure you know Mary suffered pain in childbirth. He has a different goal. Revelation 12 is not a literal description of the mystery of the nativity; it is an apocalyptic depiction of the mystery of the cross. In the words of the French New Testament scholar André Feuillet: "The messianic birth of the Apocalypse refers directly not to the birth of Christ at Bethlehem, but to the mystery of Easter morning: *the pains of childbirth correspond to Calvary*."[21]

In other words, the "anguish" of the woman in Revelation 12 is the anguish Mary experienced when she watched her son die on the hill of Golgotha.

The Gospel of John: The Woman's "Hour" and the Crucifixion

Should there be any doubt about this connection between the death of Jesus and the "birth pangs" of Mary, it is important to turn to the pages of the other book attributed to John in the New Testament: the Fourth Gospel. For Revelation is not the only book in the New Testament that uses childbirth as a metaphor for the passion and death of Christ.

In the Gospel of John, during his discourse at the Last Supper, Jesus *himself* uses the image of a "woman" who suffers in childbirth as a metaphor for his coming passion, death, and resurrection.[22] Although this mysterious passage is sometimes overlooked in discussions of Mary, it is extremely helpful for properly interpreting the meaning of the woman in labor in the book of Revelation:

> [Jesus said to his disciples:] "A little while, and you will see me no more; again a little while, and you will see me . . . Truly, truly, I say to you, you will weep and lament, but the world will rejoice; you will be sorrowful, but your sorrow will turn into joy. *When a woman gives birth she has sorrow, because her hour has come; but when she is delivered of the child, she no longer remembers the anguish, for joy that a child is born into the world.* So you have sorrow now, but I will see you again and your hearts will rejoice, and no one will take your joy from you." (John 16:16, 20–22)

Notice here that Jesus is clearly referring to his coming death ("you will see me no more") and resurrection ("you will see me"). In this context, he uses the mysterious image of a "woman" (Greek *gynē*) whose "hour" (Greek *hōra*) has come to give birth (John 16:21). While she is giving birth she will have "sorrow," but when she finally gives birth, she will not remember her "anguish" because of the "joy":

The Woman's Labor	Jesus' Crucifixion
1. Childbirth: Woman's "hour"	1. Passion: Jesus' "hour"
2. Labor Pains: she has "sorrow"	2. Death: brings "sorrow"
3. Delivery: she has "joy"	3. Resurrection: brings "joy"

As Jesus himself goes on to say, he is speaking to the disciples "in figures" (John 16:25)—that is, using metaphors. With that said, one has to ask: Isn't this a rather *strange* metaphor? Given the utter brutality of a Roman crucifixion, widely regarded as the worst possible way to die, why would Jesus choose to compare his passion and death on the cross to the "hour" of a "woman" in childbirth?

On the one hand, you could simply suggest that Jesus is using this metaphor because childbirth is indeed an intense combination of extreme suffering and extreme joy. However, I would suggest that more is going on here. In the Gospel of John, the word "hour" (Greek *hōra*) is used as a kind of technical term referring to the mystery of Christ's passion and death.[23] Furthermore, Jesus' use of the image of a woman giving birth appears to be drawing on the Jewish idea of the "birth pangs of the Messiah"—the time of suffering that will usher in the age of salvation.[24] Jesus seems to be using the metaphor of the "woman's hour" to point both to his sufferings on the cross and (in a special way) to the sufferings of Mary his mother. In support of this, look once again at John's description of the death of Jesus:

> But standing by the cross of Jesus were *his mother*, and his mother's sister, Mary the wife of Clopas, and Mary Magdalene. When Jesus saw *his mother*, and the disciple whom he loved standing near, he said to his mother, "*Woman*, behold, your son!" Then he said to the disciple, "Behold, your mother!" And from *that hour* the disciple took her to his own home. (John 19:25–27)

Did you see what just happened there? It was the fulfillment of Jesus' words at the Last Supper. Just as Jesus had compared his passion and death to the labor and sorrow of a "woman" (Greek *gynē*) whose "hour" (Greek *hōra*) of childbirth has come (John 16:21), so now the crucifixion of Jesus becomes the "hour" (Greek *hōra*) of sorrow for Mary, whom Jesus addresses as "woman" (Greek *gynē*) (John 19:26). The use of these terms is not a coincidence. Precisely because Mary is Jesus' mother, she suffers at the foot of the cross in a unique way, so that the death of Jesus becomes *her "hour"* as well—the hour of her motherly "anguish" and "sorrow" (cf. John 16:21).[25] Indeed, Jesus' prophecy about the woman's "hour" may be the only reference in the New Testament that we possess to Mary's experience of Jesus' being raised from the dead. Although she has "sorrow" now, she will have "joy" at his resurrection.

MARY'S WOMB AND JESUS' TOMB

I suspect that much of what we have covered in this chapter will come as a surprise to many readers. In my experience, most people are not aware that Jewish Scripture contains a prophecy of a woman who gives birth to the Messiah without any pain, and many are unfamiliar with the ancient Jewish belief that the age of salvation would be preceded by the "birth pangs" of the Messiah. Likewise, if my years in the classroom are any indication, virtually every student who reads Revelation's description of the woman clothed with sun crying out in the "torment" of her delivery assumes that it is a literal description of the intense birth pangs suffered by

Mary at Bethlehem. That is certainly how the labor pangs of Mary are always depicted in contemporary movies.

However, when we turn to ancient Christianity, the situation is very different. From the earliest centuries, ancient Christians believed that Isaiah's prophecy of the painless birth was fulfilled in Mary at Bethlehem. In fact, they believed that, as the new Eve and the mother of the Messiah, Mary was spared the ordinary pain of childbirth precisely because she would *not* be spared the extraordinary pain of watching her son die upon the cross. Let's bring this chapter to a close by taking a few moments to look at what ancient Christians believed about the miraculous birth of Jesus and why they thought it mattered.

The Painless Birth of Jesus: A Fulfillment of Isaiah's Prophecy

On the one hand, as I've already noted, since ancient times it has been widely believed by Christians that Mary did not suffer the pains of ordinary childbirth. In other words, both the conception and the birth of Jesus were *miraculous*. Eventually, this ancient Christian idea developed into the belief in *the virginal birth* of Christ (see CCC 499).[26]

Where did ancient Christians get such an idea? By now, the answer should be obvious: They got it from the Old Testament prophecy of the painless birth of the Messiah (Isaiah 66:7–8). Over and over again, ancient Christian writers not only affirm that the birth of Jesus was miraculous but do so because they see his birth as a fulfillment of Isaiah's prophecy. In fact, belief in the miraculous birth of Jesus goes back

to one of the earliest writings we possess after the New Testament: a book by Irenaeus of Lyons that was intended to
give a summary of the basic contents of the apostolic faith.
It is also present in the writings of other ancient Christians,
such as Gregory of Nyssa. Consider them both:

> And *concerning His birth, the same prophet [Isaiah]*
> *says in another place,* "Before she who was in labour
> gave birth, and before the birthpains came on, she
> was delivered of a male child" (Isaiah 66:7); *[thus]*
> *he indicated His unexpected and extraordinary birth*
> *from the Virgin.* (Irenaeus, *On the Apostolic Preach-*
> *ing*, 54 [2nd century A.D.])[27]

> Among the myriads of men born of Adam, suc-
> ceeding him as long as his nature will continue
> through successive births, *only [Jesus] came to light*
> *through a new way of being born . . . In fact, his birth*
> *alone occurred without labor pains,* and he alone
> began to exist without sexual relations . . . *Even*
> *the prophet Isaiah affirms that her giving birth was*
> *without pain, when he says: "Before the pangs of birth*
> *arrived, a male child came forth and was born"* (Isa
> 66:7). (Gregory of Nyssa, *On the Song of Songs* 13
> [4th century A.D.])[28]

Notice that in both examples, the belief in Mary's freedom
from birth pangs is directly based on the prophecy of the
painless birth of the Messiah in Isaiah 66. Although many

Christians nowadays may be unfamiliar with Isaiah's oracle, ancient Christians knew the Jewish Scriptures extremely well and interpreted the life of Mary in light of both the New Testament and the Old Testament.[29]

Mary Did Suffer the "Birth Pangs" of the Crucifixion

On the other hand, ancient Christian writers are equally clear that the miraculous birth of Jesus did *not* mean that Mary didn't have to suffer at all. Although Mary was spared the pangs of childbirth, she was not spared the anguish of watching her son die on the cross.

I know of no one who has expressed this belief more beautifully than the great Eastern Christian writer John Damascene. In his extremely influential book summarizing the universal and orthodox Christian faith, he has this to say:

> So far as He was born of woman, His birth was in accordance with the laws of parturition, while so far as He had no father, His birth was above the nature of generation . . . *For, as pleasure did not precede it, pain did not follow it, according to the prophet [Isaiah] who says, "Before she travailed, she brought forth, and again, before her pain came she was delivered of a man-child" (Isaiah 66:7)* . . . But just as He who was conceived kept her who conceived still virgin, in like manner also He who was born preserved her virginity intact, only passing through her and keeping her closed . . . *But this blessed woman, who*

*was deemed worthy of gifts that are supernatural, suf-
fered those pains, which she escaped at the birth, in the
hour of the passion, enduring from motherly sympathy
the rending of the bowels, and when she beheld Him,
Whom she knew to be God by the manner of His gen-
eration, killed as a malefactor, her thoughts pierced her
as a sword,* and this is the meaning of this verse:
"Yea, a sword shall pierce through thy own soul
also" (Luke 2:35). But the joy of the resurrection
transforms the pain, proclaiming Him, Who died
in the flesh, to be God. (John Damascene, *On the
Orthodox Faith,* 4.14 [8th century A.D.])[30]

Clearly, for John Damascene, the fact that Mary was spared
what so many other women throughout human history have
had to endure—with countless numbers dying in childbirth—
does not suggest that she is somehow more than human, or
that she floats above all the sufferings of this world. To the
contrary, if we take seriously both the humanity and the divinity of Jesus, then the anguish suffered by Mary as she
stood at the foot of the cross—an anguish which the book of
Revelation describes as "torment" (Revelation 12:2)—is quite
literally inconceivable. For Mary did not just watch her son
perish; she watched the one whom she knew to be the Son of
God slowly asphyxiate and die the most horrific and shame-
ful of human deaths: death on a cross.

When the crucifixion is seen in this light, one could
rightly suggest that Mary drank waters of sorrow more
deeply than any other human mother ever has. In doing

so, she has been enabled to identify with all mothers who suffer for their children. Just as Jesus is the one whom Isaiah calls the "man of sorrows" (Isaiah 53:4), so Mary as the mother of the Messiah can rightly be called the "mother of sorrows" (Latin *Mater Dolorosa*). This, as Pope John Paul II once wrote, is the deeper symbolism of the birth pangs of the woman in Revelation 12: "The woman clothed with the sun is in a certain sense identified with Mary," for the imagery of "her pangs of birth" (Revelation 12:2) "refers to the *Mother of Jesus at the Cross.*"[31]

The Meaning of the Miraculous Birth

Of course, we still have to ask, Why does any of this matter? What meaning could the painless birth of Jesus possibly have? Why was what happened to Mary's body during the birth of Jesus so important to these ancient Christian writers?

For one thing, like the virginal conception and other miracles, the virginal birth of Christ was seen as a *sign of Jesus' divinity.* Perhaps the most famous example of this idea comes from the letter of Pope Leo I which was read aloud at the second ecumenical Council of Chalcedon (A.D. 451). In this letter, Leo not only affirmed the virginal conception and birth of Jesus; he also explained why they matter. According to Leo, they are signs that Jesus is both fully human and fully divine:

> For he was conceived by the Holy Spirit within the womb of the Virgin Mother, *who gave birth to him*

in such a way that her virginity was undiminished, just as she had conceived him with her virginity undiminished ... The Son of God, therefore, descending from his heavenly throne, enters into the infirmities of this world; and, not leaving his Father's glory, he is generated in a new order and a new birth ... *Nor does the Lord Jesus Christ, born from the womb of a virgin, have a nature different from ours just because his birth was miraculous. For he who is true God is likewise true man,* and there is no falsehood in this unity, in which the lowliness of man and the height of divinity coincide ... (Pope Leo I, *The Tome to Flavian,* 2, 4 [5th century A.D.])[32]

Note well that the "miraculous birth" (Latin *nativitas mirabilis*) of Jesus in no way detracts from the fullness of his humanity. Rather, it shows forth the paradox of the incarnation itself, in which the "lowliness" of being born of a woman "coincides" with the "height" of his divinity. As we've seen with other ancient Christians, what Leo believes about Mary is based on what he believes about Jesus. Since Jesus is both fully human and fully divine, we should expect him to both enter fully into the infirmities of this world and, at the same time, to come into the world with miracles that reveal he is more than just an ordinary man.[33]

Furthermore, the miraculous birth of Jesus was seen as a *sign of the new creation.* Think about it for a minute. If, as we saw in Chapter 2, Jesus is the new Adam and Mary is the new Eve, then it is fitting that Mary would give birth to Jesus without undergoing the pain that was the result of

Eve's sin. Consider the words of two of the most influential ancient Eastern Christian writers:

> How would it have been possible for her . . . [to] give birth filled with birthpangs, in the image of the primeval curse? *If Mary was "blessed of women"* (Luke 1:42), *she would have been exempt from the curse from the beginning,* and from the bearing of children in birthpangs and curses. (Ephrem the Syrian, *Commentary on the Diatesseron,* 2.6 [4th century A.D.])[34]

> *[Christ's] birth alone occurred without labor pains,* and he alone began to exist without sexual relations . . . This happened for an understandable reason; there is nothing absurd about it. Just as she who introduced death into nature by sin was condemned to bear children in suffering and travail (Gen 3:16), it was necessary that the Mother of life, after having conceived in joy, should give birth in joy as well. (Gregory of Nyssa, *On the Song of Songs* 13 [4th century A.D.])[35]

Although modern-day people think of pain in childbirth as something "natural," this is certainly not how ancient Christians saw it. They saw it through the lens of the Jewish Bible, in which the pangs of childbirth are the result of the first sin (Genesis 3:16). Hence, just as the ancient Jews believed that in the new creation women would no longer experience birth pangs, so ancient Christians believed that the nativity of Jesus itself was the beginning of the new creation. What they believed about Mary, the second Eve, flowed directly from what they believed about Jesus, the new Adam.

Finally, and perhaps most intriguing of all, the miraculous birth of Jesus was seen as a *sign of his resurrection from the dead.* In order to see this clearly, it's important to remember two points. First—contrary to what you've probably seen in movies and artistic depictions of the resurrection—in the New Testament, the resurrected Jesus exits the tomb by *passing through the gravestone.* According to the Gospel of Matthew, when the women arrived at the tomb on Easter Sunday morning, the tomb of Jesus was still sealed. That's why "an angel from heaven" came and "rolled back the stone" (Matthew 28:2). Second, in ancient Judaism, wombs and tombs were often compared to one another. For example:

> Cursed be the man . . . [who] did not kill me in *the womb;*
> so my mother would have been *my grave,*
> and *her womb* forever great. (Jeremiah 20:15, 17)

> Much labor was created for every man,
>   and a heavy yoke is upon the sons of Adam,
> *from the day they come forth from their mother's womb,*
>   *till the day they return to the mother of all.*
>   (Sirach 40:1)

Notice that in the last line, the earth itself is given the same name as Eve: "the mother of all [the living]" (Genesis 3:22)![36]

In fact, the book of Sirach elsewhere describes death as entering into the "womb (Greek *koilias*) of Hades" (Sirach 51:5).

Once this idea of the "tomb" as a "womb" is clear, suddenly the link between the miraculous birth and the miraculous resurrection of Jesus makes sense. Although lots of examples from ancient Christian writers could be given,[37] in my opinion, two of the most striking come from the pen of Ephrem the Syrian:

> [The fact] that "they sealed the tomb" (Matt 27:66) was in [the Lord's] favour . . . He took the body out from the tomb, although it was sealed, and *the seal of the tomb* witnessed in favour of *the seal of the womb* that had borne him. For it was when the virginity was sealed that the Son emerged alive from within her . . . (Ephrem, Commentary on the Diatesseron, 21.21 [4th century A.D.])[38]

> *In your Resurrection you made your birth comprehensible; since the womb was sealed, and the sepulcher closed up* . . . The womb and the sepulcher being sealed were witnesses unto you. The womb of the Mother and hell cried aloud of your Resurrection: The womb conceived you, which was sealed; the tomb let you go forth which was closed up . . . (Ephrem, *Hymns on the Nativity*, 10.6–8 [4th century A.D.])[39]

In other words, for Ephrem, as for many other ancient Christians, the miraculous birth of Jesus from Mary's womb is not some bizarre idea—though it is a "mystery" that is ulti-mately "above the capacity of our intelligence and our words" (Severus of Antioch, *Homily* 108).[40] Instead, the miraculous birth is a *sign* that is meant to point forward to the even more miraculous exiting of the risen Jesus from the tomb! In the light of this mystery, the resurrection of Jesus becomes more than just a vindication of his power or divinity; it really is a kind of "birth," by which he becomes "the *first-born* among many brethren" (Romans 8:28).

Of course, if Jesus is the firstborn son among many sib-lings, then doesn't that suggest that Mary is not just *his* mother but *our* mother as well? To that question we will now turn, by looking at one final figure from Jewish Scripture and tradition—one who was also a woman of sorrow and joy: Rachel, the mother of Israel.

chapter 7

THE NEW RACHEL

◇◇◇◇◇

One of the great things about being a teacher is that you sometimes discover things in class, with your students, in the very act of lecturing through passages that you've read dozens of times. That's what happened to me once with the biblical story of Joseph.

The account of Joseph and his "coat of many colors" had always been one of my favorite stories in the Old Testament (see Genesis 37–50). I love it because Joseph triumphs against all odds. Just when everything seems lost—betrayed by his own brothers, sold into slavery, falsely accused and falsely imprisoned with no hope of release—God not only saves Joseph but exalts him to the highest seat in the kingdom, second only to Pharaoh himself. Eventually, when his brothers realize who Joseph is and beg for his forgiveness, he gives us the key to the whole story: "As for you, you meant evil against me; but God meant it for good, to bring it about that many people should be kept alive" (Genesis 37:20). In other words, precisely through his suffering, Joseph becomes the savior of Israel (his eleven brothers) and the Gentiles (the Egyptians).[1]

With that said, the way I understood the story of Joseph was unexpectedly transformed for me in class one day. While I was lecturing through the book of Genesis, one of the students raised her hand and asked: "Dr. Pitre, isn't the life of Joseph kind of like the life of *Jesus?*" Not wanting to appear like I didn't know this already (but not really having ever thought about it), I pulled the old professor's trick of responding with a question of my own: "That's a good question. What do you think? How is Joseph like Jesus?" As soon as I said this, something remarkable happened: One after another, the students began pointing out all kinds of parallels between the life of Joseph in the Old Testament and the life of Jesus in the New Testament—parallels that I had never noticed before. Here is some of what I wrote on the board that day:

The Life of Joseph	The Life of Jesus
1. Joseph is the firstborn son of Rachel and the beloved son of Jacob. (Genesis 30:22–24, 37:3)	1. Jesus is the firstborn son of Mary and the beloved Son of God (Matthew 1:25, 3:17)
2. Joseph is sold to the Gentiles for twenty silver pieces by Judah, one of twelve brothers. (Genesis 37:25–36)	2. Jesus is sold to the Gentiles for thirty silver pieces by Judas, one of the twelve disciples. (Matthew 26:15, 30)

3. Joseph is with two condemned men (cupbearer and baker), one of whom is pardoned and given physical life. (Genesis 40:1–23)

3. Jesus is with two condemned men, one of whom is forgiven by Jesus and given everlasting life. (Luke 23:32, 39–43)

4. Joseph is "thirty years old" when he enters Pharaoh's service. (Genesis 41:46)

4. Jesus is "thirty years old" when he begins his ministry. (Luke 3:23)

5. Joseph is exalted to the right hand of Pharaoh, rules over the kingdom of Egypt. (Genesis 41:40–44)

5. Jesus is exalted to the right hand of God, rules over the kingdom of heaven. (Acts 2:32–33)

6. Joseph saves Israel and the Gentiles from death and feeds them life-giving wheat. (Genesis 41:55–57)

6. Jesus saves Israel and the Gentiles from spiritual death and feeds them eternal life-giving bread. (John 6)

7. Joseph gives special honor to Benjamin, youngest of the twelve, at a banquet. (Genesis 43:33–34)

7. Jesus gives special honor to the Beloved Disciple, at the Last Supper. (John 13:23)

8. Joseph is revealed to his brothers, who do not recognize him at first, after he is exalted to the throne of Egypt. (Genesis 42:8)

8. Jesus is revealed to his disciples, who do not recognize him at first, after he is raised from the dead. (Luke 24)

The effect of these parallels on the class (and on me) was mesmerizing. It was like we had uncovered a great secret together. I went home that day stunned that, after all these years of studying the Old and New Testaments, it had never even occurred to me to consider that, in addition to being a new Adam, a new Moses, and a new David, Jesus might also be a new Joseph.

As soon as I got back to my office, I began to do some research, and sure enough, I quickly learned that ancient Christian writers had recognized the parallels between Joseph and Jesus. To take just one example: In the fourth century A.D., the Persian Christian writer Aphrahat the Sage wrote an entire explanation of how, in the Old Testament, *"Joseph who was persecuted was a type of the persecuted Jesus"* (Aphrahat, *Demonstration* 21.9).[2] So much for our "discovery"! As I soon learned, both ancient Christian writers and modern-day scholars have shown that "Joseph is one of the most striking biblical types of Jesus."[3]

What does any of this have to do with Mary? The answer lies with *Rachel,* the mother of Joseph. In this chapter, I will argue that the New Testament not only depicts Jesus as a new Joseph but also draws several fascinating connections between Mary and Rachel. Indeed, if we can begin to see Mary as the *new Rachel,* we will also begin to understand why it is that ancient Christians thought of Mary not only as the biological mother of Jesus but as the spiritual mother of the Church, and a powerful intercessor with God in heaven. As we will learn, to this very day, Rachel is honored by Jews and Muslims alike, and the site of Rachel's tomb is visited by devout Jews who believe in the power of her prayers of intercession.[4]

In order to see all this clearly, we will have to go back one last time and familiarize ourselves with what ancient Jewish Scripture and tradition had to say about Rachel's role in the history of her people.

RACHEL IN ANCIENT JUDAISM

As with all the patriarchs and matriarchs in the Old Testament, beliefs about Rachel at the time of Jesus would have been shaped by what the Jewish Bible had to say about her and by developments in later Jewish tradition. Hence, before we can look at the connections between Rachel and Mary in the New Testament, we need to be sure that we are familiar with what the Old Testament and other ancient Jewish writings have to tell us about Rachel.

Rachel in the Old Testament: Mother of Joseph and Benjamin

When we turn to the pages of the Jewish Bible, four aspects of the portrait of Rachel in the Old Testament stand out as important for understanding the portrait of Mary in the New Testament.[5]

The first thing to know about Rachel—whose Hebrew name means "female sheep" or "ewe"—is that she was the beloved wife of Jacob, the father of the twelve tribes of Israel (Genesis 29:28–30). The Bible emphasizes that Rachel was blessed with great physical beauty—she was "beautiful and lovely"—and that Jacob did truly love her (Genesis 29:17, 20).[6] Nevertheless, Rachel's life was filled with suffering. From the beginning of her marriage, she underwent many hardships. Not only did her father, Laban, trick Jacob into marrying her older sister, Leah, but once Rachel finally was married to Jacob, she discovered that she was barren (Genesis 30:1). As a result, she and Leah became locked in a struggle for favor in their husband's eyes, and both of them ended up giving their maidservants to Jacob so that he might father more children through them (Genesis 30:1–13). That is how Jacob ended up with twelve sons. He fathered six of them through his wife Leah, two of them through Leah's maid Zilpah, two of them through Rachel's maid Bilhah, and then, finally, two of them through Rachel herself (see Genesis 29:31–30:24).

Second, Rachel was the *biological mother of Joseph*, the eleventh of Jacob's sons but the firstborn son of the wife he loved. As the book of Genesis tells us:

> Then God remembered Rachel, and God heark-
> ened to her and *opened her womb*. She conceived
> and bore a son, and said, "God has taken away my
> reproach"; and *she called his name Joseph*, saying,
> "May the LORD add to me another son!" (Genesis
> 30:22–24)

Once you understand that Joseph was the firstborn son of Rachel, the entire story of the coat of many colors makes sense. The reason Jacob favored Joseph and gave him the special garment was that in Jacob's eyes, Joseph was the *firstborn son of Rachel*, the wife he had always loved. And the reason the ten older brothers envied Joseph was that in their eyes, he was simply the eleventh son and had no right to any special role or inheritance:

Zilpah —— Leah ——— Jacob — Rachel ———Bilhah

Zilpah	Leah		Rachel	Bilhah
7. Gad	1. Reuben		11. *Joseph*	5. Dan
8. Asher	2. Simeon		12. Benjamin	6. Naphtali
	3. Levi			
	4. Judah			
	9. Issachar			
	10. Zebulum			

As this chart makes clear, the entire story of Joseph in the Old Testament hinges on one fact: that he was the firstborn son of Rachel.

Third, Rachel *dies while giving birth to Benjamin*, the twelfth son of Jacob and the only full brother of Joseph. In one of the most poignant stories in the Bible, we read:

> Then they journeyed from Bethel; and when they were still some distance from Ephrath, *Rachel travailed, and she had hard labor.* And when she was in her hard labor, the midwife said to her, "Fear not; for now you will have another son." *And as her soul was departing (for she died), she called his name Benoni; but his father called his name Benjamin.* So Rachel died, and she was buried on the way to Ephrath

(that is, *Bethlehem*), and Jacob set up a pillar upon her grave; it is the pillar of *Rachel's tomb, which is there to this day.* (Genesis 35:16–20)

Notice the meaning of the Hebrew names given to the child. Although Rachel names the boy "Son of my sorrow" (Hebrew *Ben-'oni*), Jacob changes his name to something more positive: "Son of my right hand" (Hebrew *Binyamin*) (Genesis 35:18). Notice also that Rachel is not buried with the other mothers of Israel (Sarah, Rebekah) in the family tomb; instead, she is buried on the road near "Bethlehem" (Genesis 35:19). Intriguingly, the author of Genesis makes clear that the location of the tomb is known "to this day."

Fourth and finally, Rachel is not just the mother of Joseph and Benjamin. She is also the *mother of all Israel*, who somehow suffers with them and weeps for them, *even after her death.* Consider the mysterious oracle in the book of Jeremiah that depicts Rachel as weeping for her "children" who have been killed and driven out of the promised land and into exile:

> Thus says the LORD:
> "A voice is heard in Ramah,
> lamentation and bitter weeping.
> *Rachel is weeping for her children;*
> *she refuses to be comforted for her children,*
> because they are not." (Jeremiah 31:15)

What are we to make of this passage? How can Jeremiah say that Rachel is weeping for the exiles of Israel in the sixth century B.C. when she has been dead and buried for centuries? According to Old Testament scholars, the key to understanding this passage is to remember that Rachel's tomb was located near the place where the exiles were taken captive by the Babylonians.[7] In other words, Jeremiah depicts "the spirit" of Rachel as still living, witnessing the suffering of her descendants, and acting as "the classic mother who mourns and intercedes for her children."[8] Indeed, it is precisely her intercession that succeeds in moving the heart of God. For in the very next verse, God tells Rachel not to cry anymore because her "work" will be "rewarded," and her children will come back to the promised land (Jeremiah 31:16–17).

Rachel in Jewish Tradition: The Most Powerful Intercessor

So much for the portrait of Rachel in Jewish Scripture. When we turn to later traditions about Rachel outside the Bible, three things stand out as potentially important for understanding Mary in the New Testament.[9]

First, Rachel was remembered as a woman of intense suffering. As Josephus tells us in his history of Israel, not only did Rachel die "in childbirth" but her son was called Benjamin "because of the suffering (Greek *odynē*) which he had caused his mother" (Josephus, *Antiquities* 1.344).[10]

Second, the geographical link between Rachel's tomb and the *city of Bethlehem* continued to be preserved in Jewish writings down to the first century and beyond. For example, the ancient Jewish writer Demetrius the Chronographer (3rd century B.C.) tells us that Jacob came "to Ephrath, which is

Bethlehem, and there he fathered Benjamin; and Rachel died after giving birth to Benjamin" (Demetrius, *Chronography*, 2.10).[11] Along similar lines, one later rabbinic tradition actually says that the reason Jacob buried Rachel at that particular spot is that "Jacob foresaw that the exiles would pass on from thence, therefore he buried her *so that she might pray mercy for them*" (*Genesis Rabbah* 82:10).[12] Down through the centuries, Jews, Christians, and Muslims have come to regard the traditional site of Rachel's tomb near the city of Bethlehem as a holy place of prayer. (In the twentieth century, we even have records of Jews visiting Rachel's tomb to light candles and ask for her prayers!)[13]

Third and finally, in the ancient rabbinic commentaries, Rachel is depicted not just as the "matriarch" of her people but as the *most powerful intercessor* on behalf of Israel. For example, in one tradition, both Abraham and Moses come to God weeping and pleading for Israel after the destruction of the Temple in Jerusalem, but God does not answer their prayers (*Lamentations Rabbah* 24).[14] It is only when the "matriarch Rachel" intercedes with God on behalf of the sinful people that he responds:

> Forthwith the mercy of the Holy One, blessed be He, was stirred, and He said, *"For your sake, Rachel, I will restore Israel to their place"*. And so it is written, "Thus says the Lord: A voice is heard in Ramah, lamentation and bitter weeping, Rachel weeping for her children; she refuses to be comforted for her children, because they are not" (Jer 31:15). This

is followed by, "Thus says the Lord: Refrain your
voice from weeping, and your eyes from tears; for
your work shall be rewarded . . . and there is hope
for your future, says the Lord; and your children
shall return to their own border." (Jer 31:16) (*Lamentations Rabbah* 24)[15]

Notice here that the belief that Rachel's intercession was su-
premely effective is directly based on the prophecy of Jeremiah that we looked at previously (Jeremiah 31:15–18). As
the modern-day Jewish scholar Jacob Neusner points out,
the logic of this rabbinic tradition is straightforward. In
response to the depths of her motherly sorrow, Rachel's intercession with God "succeeds when all other intervention
fails," because "she speaks not of sacrifice but of love."[16]

In sum, although Rachel may not be the most well-known
woman of the Old Testament in contemporary Christian cir-
cles, the same thing was not true in ancient Judaism. As the
wife of Jacob/Israel himself, Rachel was regarded in a special
way as the *sorrowful mother* of all Israel, whose special role
was to pray for and intercede on behalf of her children, even
though she was no longer here on earth.

MARY THE NEW RACHEL

With all of this Jewish background in mind, when we open
the pages of the New Testament, we discover several fascinating but often overlooked links between the figure of Rachel and Mary, the mother of Jesus.

The Massacre of the Infants: Rachel, Mary, and Their Children

The first and most explicit connection between Rachel in the Old Testament and Mary in the New Testament comes in the famous story of King Herod's massacre of the infant children in Bethlehem. Although the story is well known, read it again in light of everything we've learned so far about the figure of Rachel in ancient Judaism:

> Then Herod, when he saw that he had been tricked by the wise men, was in a furious rage, and he sent and killed *all the male children in Bethlehem and in all that region* who were two years old or under, according to the time which he had ascertained from the wise men. *Then was fulfilled what was spoken by the prophet Jeremiah: "A voice was heard in Ramah, wailing and loud lamentation, Rachel weeping for her children;* she refused to be consoled, because they were no more." But when Herod died, behold, an angel of the Lord appeared in a dream to Joseph in Egypt, saying, "Rise, *take the child and his mother,* and go to the land of Israel, for those who sought the child's life are dead." And he rose and took *the child and his mother,* and went to the land of Israel. (Matthew 2:16–21, quoting Jeremiah 31:15)

Notice three things about this mysterious and tragic event.

First and foremost, the massacre of the infants happens in the vicinity of Rachel's tomb. Just as Rachel is buried on

the road "to Bethlehem" (Genesis 35:19), so the children who
are slaughtered by Herod are from "Bethlehem" and the sur-
rounding "region" (Matthew 2:16).[17]

Second, although Rachel has died, she is somehow aware
of the sufferings of her descendants, and she laments for them
as the mother of Israel. That is why Matthew quotes Jeremiah's prophecy of "Rachel weeping for her children" (Matthew
2:18; Jeremiah 31:15). In the words of one Protestant scholar:
"Rachel, who wept from her grave in Bethlehem during the
captivity [of the exile], was now weeping at another, nearer
crisis significant in salvation history."[18] Intriguingly, Matthew seems to share the Jewish belief that Rachel, though
long dead, is not oblivious to the sufferings of her descendants. She knows what is taking place on earth and grieves
for them.

Third and finally, as the contemporary Jewish scholar
David Flusser has pointed out, insofar as they both suffer
for their children, Rachel and Mary are counterparts of each
other: "In Matthew, *Rachel is a symbolic figure for the suffering mother*, in this case, the suffering Jewish mother. And
Rachel's pain for the dead children is also symbolic for *the
suffering of Mary* in relation to her illustrious son."[19] Along
similar lines, the Jewish scholar Jacob Neusner describes
Rachel as "Mary's ancient Israelite counterpart."[20] In other
words, as the suffering mother of the persecuted child who is
driven into exile, Mary in Matthew's Gospel is truly a *new
Rachel*. Indeed, on a very human level, it is easy to imagine
Mary weeping not only for the persecution and exile of her
own son but for the lives of all the boys who were massacred
in the attempt to kill her child.

The Book of Revelation: The Woman with the Sun, Moon, and Stars

The second link between Rachel and Mary takes place in John's vision of the woman clothed with the sun (Revelation 12:1–6). As should be clear by now, there are multiple layers of symbolism in this complex apocalyptic vision, which can be peeled away only by looking at the Old Testament passages to which John alludes, whether they be of Eve, or the Ark, or the queen mother.

At this point in our study, you might be tempted to think we've exhausted all of the biblical background to Revelation 12. Yet there remains one more passage that lies behind the vision. Reread it one last time, this time focusing on a different set of images drawn from the Old Testament:

> And a great portent appeared in heaven, *a woman clothed with the sun*, with *the moon* under her feet, and on her head a crown of *twelve stars*; she was with child and *she cried out in her pangs of birth*, in anguish for delivery. (Revelation 12:1–3)

Several aspects of this vision point us back to Rachel, the mother of all Israel.

For one thing, as scholars widely recognize, the vision of the woman in heaven is *directly based on the dream of Joseph*, in which the sun, moon, and stars symbolize Jacob, Rachel, and their eleven sons:[21]

> Then [Joseph] dreamed another dream, and told it to his brothers, and said, "Behold, I have dreamed

another dream; and behold, *the sun, the moon, and eleven stars were bowing down to me.*" But when he told it to his father and to his brothers, his father rebuked him, and said to him, "What is this dream that you have dreamed? Shall *I* and *your mother* and *your brothers* indeed come to bow ourselves to the ground before you?" And his brothers were jealous of him, but his father kept the saying in mind. (Genesis 37:9–11)

Notice here that in Joseph's dream, the "moon" very clearly stands for Rachel his "mother" (Genesis 37:9–10).[22] When we remember that in the Jewish Bible, putting something or someone "under one's feet" is often an image for royal dominion (e.g., Psalms 8:7; 110:1–4), the implication of John's vision of a woman who is clothed with the sun, standing on the moon, and wearing a crown of twelve stars seems to be that the heavenly Mother of the Messiah is exalted above all Israel, including the patriarchs and matriarchs of old.

Moreover, as any first-century Jew would have known, the image of a woman "crying out in her pangs of birth (Greek *ōdinousa*) in anguish for delivery" (Revelation 12:2) could easily call to mind the one woman whose anguish in childbirth is explicitly described in the Jewish Bible: Rachel. As we just saw, both Jewish Scripture and later tradition remembered that Rachel suffered "hard labor" and that her "pain" (Greek *odynē*) was so severe that she died in childbirth (Genesis 37:15 LXX; Josephus, *Antiquities* 1.344). Indeed, in the ancient Greek Septuagint, Benjamin's name is actually "Son of my pain" (Greek *odynē*) (Genesis 35:18 LXX).

Last—and this is significant—the woman clothed with the sun is not just the mother of the Messiah. She is also the mother of *all* the children of God. John is very explicit about this: "The dragon was angry with the woman, and went off to make war on *the rest of her offspring*, on those who keep the commandments of God and bear testimony to Jesus" (Revelation 12:17). Just as Rachel was regarded in a special way as the mother of all God's persecuted children in the Old Testament (Jeremiah 31:15), so the heavenly woman clothed with the sun is mother to all those who believe in Jesus but are persecuted by the forces of evil.[23]

The Mother of Jesus and the "Beloved" Disciple

The third and final connection between Mary and Rachel may be the most subtle of all, but it is also potentially the most significant. Although I do not know of any New Testament scholar who has recognized the parallel, I would suggest that Mary is also being depicted as a new Rachel in the Gospel of John, insofar as she becomes the mother of the Beloved Disciple through her suffering at Golgotha.

Although we have also studied this passage before, consider one more time John's account of the crucifixion of Jesus, this time focusing your attention on Mary's becoming the mother of the Beloved Disciple:

> So the soldiers did this. But standing by the cross
> of Jesus were his mother, and his mother's sister,
> Mary the wife of Clopas, and Mary Magdalene.
> When Jesus saw *his mother*, and *the disciple whom he*

loved standing near, he said to his mother, *"Woman, behold, your son!"* Then he said to the disciple, *"Behold, your mother!"* And from that hour the disciple took her to his own home. (John 19:25–27)

In order to see the connections between Rachel and Mary at the foot of the cross, several points need to be kept in mind.

To begin with, as we saw in Chapter 6, Jesus himself compares his crucifixion to the sorrow of a woman in childbirth (John 16:21–22). For any ancient Jew familiar with the Scriptures, the image of a sorrowing mother giving birth would easily call to mind Rachel's sorrowful delivery of her second son, Benjamin (Genesis 35:16–20).

In addition, just as Rachel gave birth to her second-born son, Benjamin, through suffering and dying in childbirth, so Mary spiritually "gives birth" to her second son—the Beloved Disciple—by her interior suffering and "dying" at the foot of the cross. It's crucial to remember here that the prophet Simeon describes Mary's future sufferings at the cross as having her "soul" pierced by "a sword"—in other words, as a kind of "spiritual death":

> Simeon . . . said *to Mary his mother,*
> "Behold, this child is set for the fall and rising of
>   many in Israel,
> and for a sign that is spoken against;
> *and a sword will pierce through your own soul also,*
> that thoughts out of many hearts may be revealed."
>   (Luke 2:34–35)[24]

In other words, just as Rachel's "soul" (Greek *psychē*) departed and she "died" giving birth to Benjamin (Genesis 35:18 LXX), so Mary's "soul" (Greek *psychē*) is slain by the "sword" of the suffering she experiences at the foot of the cross (Luke 2:35).[25] Mary's suffering, like Rachel's, is not futile but fruitful. For it is precisely *through* her interior dying that she becomes the mother of another child: the apostle John.

Perhaps most intriguing of all, if Mary is being depicted as a new Rachel and the apostle John as a kind of "new Benjamin," then this would provide an explanation for the otherwise baffling question of why the author of John's Gospel refers to himself as the "Beloved Disciple" (cf. John 13:23; 19:26; 21:7; 21:20). For decades, contemporary scholars have struggled to come up with a convincing explanation for why John refers to himself in this enigmatic (and seemingly prideful!) way.[26] I suggest that the solution to the riddle lies in the Old Testament and in the fact that Jesus gives Mary to John to be his mother. Should there be any doubt about this, notice that in one of the most famous passages in the Jewish Bible—the last testament of Moses—Benjamin the son of Rachel is identified not just as the younger brother of Joseph but as "the beloved" of God:

> Of *Benjamin* he said, "*The beloved of the LORD,*
> he dwells in safety by him; he encompasses him all
> the day long,
> and makes his dwelling between his shoulders." (Deuteronomy 33:12)

Just as Benjamin is the "beloved (Greek *ēgapēmenos*) of the LORD" (Deuteronomy 33:12), so John is the "disciple whom Jesus loved (Greek *ēgapa*)" (John 19:26). By referring to himself as the "beloved disciple," John indicates that he takes the same position amongst the twelve apostles that Benjamin once took among the twelve sons of Jacob: the "beloved" younger son of Rachel and brother of Joseph:

Old Testament	New Testament
1. Rachel	1. Mary
2. Joseph: firstborn son of Rachel	2. Jesus: firstborn son of Mary
3. Benjamin: "son" of Rachel's "sorrow"	3. John: "son" of Mary's "sorrow"
4. 12 Sons: Benjamin is "beloved"	4. 12 Apostles: John is "beloved"

In other words, just as Benjamin was specially loved by Joseph because they were both sons of Rachel, so John is specially "loved" by Jesus because *they have the same mother.* Just as Joseph was the firstborn son of Rachel in the Old Testament, so Jesus is the firstborn son of Mary in the New Testament. And just as Benjamin was the "son" of Rachel's "sorrow," because she had to die to give birth to him, so John becomes the "son" of Mary's sorrow, because Mary becomes his mother only through the anguish and "sorrow" that she experiences at the foot of the cross.

MOTHER OF THE CHURCH

What is the significance of these connections between Mary and Rachel? If Mary really is being revealed as the new Rachel of the New Covenant, then at least three important implications follow.

Mother of All Disciples

If Rachel was indeed the "matriarch" of her people—the mother of all Israel (Jeremiah 31:15), then it seems clear that Mary, the new Rachel, is the "matriarch" of the entire Church. This is the only plausible explanation for why the book of Revelation describes all those who "bear testimony to Jesus" as "offspring" of the mother of the Messiah (Revelation 12:17, cf. 1–6). Just as Rachel was regarded as the mother of all Israel in the Old Covenant, so Mary becomes the mother of the Church in the New Covenant.

This spiritual motherhood of Mary with relationship to the Church as a whole is something that has been recognized since the early centuries of Christianity. Consider, for example, the words of Ambrose of Milan, when he speaks of the deeper meaning of Jesus' act of giving Mary to John to be his mother:

> *"May the Christ from the height of the cross say also to each of you: 'There is your mother.'* May he say also to the Church: 'There is your son.'" (Ambrose, *On Luke* 7.5 [4th century A.D.])[27]

Clearly, since ancient times Christians have recognized that if Jesus gave Mary to the Beloved Disciple to be *his* mother, then this means that, in some way, he also gave Mary to *all* his disciples. Indeed, the idea of Mary's spiritual maternity with reference to the Church is not something "made up" by Catholics in the Middle Ages; it is something that flows directly out of the will of Jesus as expressed to his mother and John while Jesus was hanging on the cross.

In much more recent times, Pope John Paul II expressed the same idea of Mary's motherhood with relation to the Church, emphasizing that it is precisely through her sharing in the cross of Christ that she, in a sense, "gave birth" not only to John as her "second-born" son but also to the Church as a whole:

> *On Calvary, Mary united herself to the sacrifice of her Son and made her own maternal contribution to the work of salvation,* which took the form of labour pains, the birth of the new humanity. In addressing the words "Woman, behold your son" to Mary, the Crucified One proclaims her motherhood not only in relation to the Apostle John but also to every disciple. The Evangelist himself, by saying that Jesus had to die "to gather into one the children of God who are scattered abroad" (Jn. 11:52), indicates *the Church's birth as the fruit of the redemptive sacrifice with which Mary is maternally associated.* (Pope John Paul II, General Audience, September 17, 1997)[28]

In other words, Mary is not the mother of the Church because she happens to be the biological mother of Jesus. She is the mother of the Church because she willingly consented to and shared in the sufferings of Christ on the cross, through which the redemption of the world is accomplished.

Mother of Sorrows

If Mary is the new Rachel, then she may truly be described as the "mother of sorrows" (Latin *Mater Dolorosa*). Just as Rachel was seen as having a uniquely maternal role toward Israel because of the sorrows she suffered during her life and, even more, after her death (Jeremiah 31:15–17), so Mary can be seen as having a uniquely maternal role precisely because of the sorrows that she suffered as the mother of Jesus at the foot of the cross.

In this case, the words of the contemporary Jewish scholar David Flusser strike a powerful note:

> Mary can be understood as a symbol for the church and also for her own people. But one should never forget that this woman once walked the earth— this mother of sorrows. The Mater Dolorosa is not a theological concept or an overpowering experience of the archetypal but primarily a real person who was inspired by her joy and never defeated by her unspeakable pain.[29]

Flusser has put his finger here on a very important point. In this book, we've seen lots of remarkable connections between the Old and New Testaments, and (I hope) shed some important light on key Christian doctrines and practices regarding the mother of Jesus. But at the end of the day, it's important to remember that *Mary is not a doctrine or a dogma, but a person.* She was a real, living human being who, like all of us, had to walk the long journey through this valley of tears.

However exalted her status may be as the new Eve, the new Ark, the new queen mother, et cetera, Mary is still a human woman who knew what it was to suffer and have sorrow. That is what makes her such an amazingly appealing figure in the history of Christianity; when it comes to suffering, sorrow, and death, *Mary knows what it is like* to endure excruciating pain—the kind of interior pain that can be described only as having one's "soul" pierced "by a sword" (Luke 2:35). Indeed, since Mary becomes our mother precisely through what she suffered at the foot the cross, we can truly say that *we are the children of Mary's sorrow.*

A Maternal Intercessor in Heaven

Finally, if Mary is the new Rachel, then she, like Rachel before her, must be a powerful intercessor indeed.

Recall here that in ancient Jewish tradition Rachel was regarded as the most powerful intercessor with God on behalf of her children on earth. In the same way, if Mary is truly the mother of all disciples, then there is no reason to think she abandons her maternal relationship with the Church on earth just because her earthly life comes to an end. Indeed, as we saw in Chapter 3, if Mary was assumed bodily into the heavenly Temple to be with the risen Jesus forever, then she is most certainly *not "dead."* Mary is *a living intercessor;* she is much more alive than any human on earth.

Perhaps this is why, as we saw in Chapter 3, we have ancient Christian prayers in which Mary is addressed not only as "Mother of God" (Greek *Theotokos*) but as the "refuge" of her suffering children on earth:

> We take refuge in your mercy, Mother of God. *Do not disregard our prayers in troubling times, but deliver us from danger,* O only pure one, only blessed one. (Anonymous Christian Prayer [3rd–4th century A.D.])[30]

Notice that the ancient Christians who composed this prayer asked Mary to pray for them especially in the midst of "troubling times" and "danger": both likely allusions to the bloody persecutions of Christians that were known in the early centuries of the Church in Egypt.

More recently, in 1964, the Second Vatican Council beautifully expressed this same idea. In its document on the Church, Vatican II taught that although Mary no longer lives in this world, she *never stops interceding* for her spiritual children on earth:

> The motherhood of Mary in the order of grace continues uninterruptedly from the consent which she loyally gave at the Annunciation and which she sustained without wavering beneath the cross, until the eternal fulfillment of all the elect. Taken

up into heaven she did not lay aside this saving office but by her manifold intercession continues to
bring us the gifts of eternal salvation. By her maternal charity, she cares for the brethren of her Son,
who still journey on earth surrounded by dangers
and difficulties, until they are led into their blessed
home. (Vatican II, *Lumen Gentium*, 62)[31]

It is striking to find this sentiment expressed at Vatican II
also in the words of the contemporary Jewish scholar Jacob
Neusner. In a truly remarkable essay, Neusner once noted
that Mary's role as a powerful intercessor on behalf of Christians made perfect sense to him given the parallels between
Rachel in Judaism and Mary in Christianity:

> That is why I can find in Mary a Christian, *a Cath-*
> *olic Rachel*, whose prayers count when the prayers
> of great men, fathers of the world, fall to the
> ground . . . No wonder that, when Rachel weeps,
> God listens. How hard, then, can it be for me to
> find in Mary that sympathetic, special friend that
> Catholics have known for 2,000 years! Not so hard
> at all. So, yes, if Rachel, then why not Mary?[32]

In other words, from a Jewish perspective, the idea that God
would give a special place and power to the prayers of a loving and sorrowful mother is not only plausible but compelling. If God listens to the weeping of Rachel, the mother of
his beloved children of Israel, then surely he will also listen

to the weeping of Mary, the sorrowful mother of his only-begotten Son and the spiritual mother of all of the disciples of Jesus, especially those who are suffering and persecuted in this world.

At least, that is what Jesus himself seems to suggest when he says to John the disciple: "Behold, your mother." Let's bring this book to a close by turning our attention to these words—the last words of Jesus spoken to his disciples before he died.

chapter 8

AT THE FOOT OF THE CROSS

◇◇◇◇◇

There is something inescapably sacred about a person's last words. If you've ever had the experience of being with someone you love in his or her last moments, then you know what I'm talking about. Whether the dying person is your mother or father, your sister or brother, your wife or husband, your child or your best friend—if you get the chance to hear them speak, *you do not forget* the last things they say. Last words reveal the heart of a person: who and what mattered to them in this world, and what they thought most important to say before passing over into the silence of death.

The same thing is true of Jesus' last words from the cross. They matter too, because they reveal his heart, who and what mattered to him, and what he thought most important to say in the last moments of his earthly life. In this final chapter, I want to bring our journey to a close by focusing on what Jesus said about Mary before he died on the cross. Although we've looked at John's account of Jesus' death more than once, consider it one last time:

> But standing by the cross of Jesus were his mother, and his mother's sister, Mary the wife of Clopas, and Mary Magdalene. *When Jesus saw his mother, and the disciple whom he loved standing near, he said to his mother, "Woman, behold, your son!" Then he said to the disciple, "Behold, your mother!" And from that hour the disciple took her to his own home.* After this Jesus, knowing that all was now finished, said (to fulfil the scripture), "I thirst." A bowl full of vinegar stood there; so they put a sponge full of the vinegar on hyssop and held it to his mouth. When Jesus had received the vinegar, he said, "It is finished"; and he bowed his head and gave up his spirit. (John 19:25–30)

According to the Gospels, Jesus speaks seven times from the cross; but these are the only words that are directly addressed to a follower of his. What are we to make of them? Given the fact that crucifixion was basically death by asphyxiation, why would Jesus willingly suffer the excruciating pain it would have caused him to pull himself up by the nails in his hands and feet and utter these words to his mother and his disciple?[1] What does Jesus mean when he says, "behold, your son," and "behold, your mother"?

JESUS' LAST WORDS

On the level of the historical meaning of the words, the answer is straightforward but significant.

First, Jesus' words to Mary and the Beloved Disciple are a kind of formal *last will and testament*. As biblical scholars have pointed out, in the ancient world, a man sentenced to death by execution was legally able to bequeath his possessions by simply declaring his will from the cross.[2] When it comes to Jesus, of course, he has no possessions: no money, no land, and no home to give away. He doesn't even have any clothes, since the soldiers have already stripped him of his garments and divided them among themselves by casting lots (John 19:23–24). Thus, the only earthly "possession" Jesus has left is his mother. *And he even gives her away.* As a result, he dies in complete poverty.

Second, Jesus' last words to Mary and John are a kind of formal act of adoption, by which Mary takes John to be her adopted son, and John takes Mary to be his adoptive mother. In the words of one Protestant scholar:

> From the cross, Jesus sees his mother and the Beloved Disciple standing nearby and, with a simple statement, gives the Beloved Disciple as a son to his mother and gives his mother to the Beloved Disciple. By this ceremonial act, *a new relationship is formed; a new family is created.*[3]

In ancient Judaism, adoptive relationships were real; they were legally binding. (Think here of the genealogy of Joseph and his adoptive fatherhood toward Jesus.)[4] In other words, Jesus is not just expressing a fleeting wish on his part for someone to "look after" Mary once he has died. He is making a formal declaration of his will: Mary really becomes John's mother and John really becomes Mary's son.

Third and finally, lest there be any doubt about this, it is important to emphasize the Beloved Disciple's response: "From that hour the disciple *took her to his own home*" (John 19:27). On one level, this means that the Beloved Disciple took Mary to live with him—a point that is corroborated by the fact that after the resurrection, when the apostles are gathered together in Jerusalem awaiting Pentecost, "Mary the mother of Jesus" is there with them (Acts 1:14). On the other hand, the original Greek of John's Gospel does not use the ordinary word for "home" (Greek *oikos*). What John actually says is that he took Mary "to his own" (Greek *eis ta idia*) (John 19:27). The Greek word *idia* is "a broader term that means one's 'own,'" as in one's own family, people, or possessions (e.g., John 1:11; Luke 18:28–29).[5] In other words, the Beloved Disciple is *to treat Mary as his mother.* By accepting Jesus' last will and testament, the mother of Jesus is now John's own mother and he is now her own son.

In sum, according to the New Testament, the fate of Mary his mother was one of the things that mattered most to Jesus during his last moments on the cross. Only once he has given Mary away to the Beloved Disciple can it be said that "all was now finished" (John 19:28). Only after he has given Mary to John does he lay down his life: "He bowed his head and gave up his spirit" (John 19:30).

HE TOOK HER TO BE HIS OWN

But this is not the only meaning of Jesus' words. Since ancient times, the Gospel of John has been referred to as the "spiritual Gospel."[6] One reason is that in it there's almost always a deeper spiritual meaning to Jesus' words and actions. From this point of view, the last words of Jesus to Mary and John—"Behold, your son . . . Behold, your mother" (John 19:25, 27)—take on a deeper significance.

For one thing, in the Gospel of John, the Beloved Disciple is an "ideal figure."[7] He is not just a historical follower of Jesus; in a certain sense, he symbolizes what every true "disciple" should aspire to be.[8] As Jesus himself says at the Last Supper: "By this my Father is glorified, that you bear much fruit, and so prove to be *my disciples.* As the Father has loved me, so *I have loved you;* abide in my love" (John 15:8–9). In other words, every true "disciple" is called to be a "beloved" disciple. Indeed, one plausible reason the author of John's Gospel does not use the Beloved Disciple's name is that he wants the reader to see himself or herself in the figure of the disciple "whom Jesus loved" (John 13:23).

If this is correct, then when Jesus speaks his last words to the Beloved Disciple from the cross, in a certain sense, he is also speaking to every disciple. Jesus is saying to each one of his followers: "Behold, your mother." As one Protestant commentator on the Gospel of John writes:

> Mary, the Mother of the Lord, becomes *the mother of the faithful,* and the Beloved Disciple here seems to denote *the ideal Christian* convert.[9]

Notice that this new relationship with Mary is not based on biology or blood; it is created through the passion and death of Jesus. It is the suffering of his "hour" that makes Mary our mother.[10] We are the children of the "birth pangs" she experienced at the foot of the cross (cf. John 16:20–21; Revelation 12:1–6). As John says at the beginning of his Gospel: "To all who received him, who believed in his name, he gave power to become children of God; who were born, not of blood nor of the will of the flesh, nor of the will of man, but of God" (John 1:12–13).

Finally, and most important of all, if every disciple is called to imitate the Beloved Disciple, then Jesus is *inviting every Christian to take Mary to be his or her own mother.* This, at least, is the most ancient interpretation of Jesus' last words that we possess. In his famous commentary on the Gospel of John, Origen of Alexandria writes:

> The firstfruits of the Gospels is that according to John, whose meaning no one can understand who has not leaned on Jesus' breast nor received Mary from Jesus to be his mother also. (Origen, *Commentary on John*, 1.23 [3rd century A.D.])[11]

In other words, Jesus is inviting all of his disciples to enter into a *personal relationship with Mary* as their own spiritual mother. His dying wish is for Mary to become the mother of all Christians, not just of the Beloved Disciple.

BEHOLD, YOUR MOTHER

But what happens when you do this? What happens when you choose not to ignore or dismiss Mary but to really "behold" her? What happens when you take Jesus' dying words to heart, imitate the Beloved Disciple, and take Mary to be your own mother?

I'll tell you what happens: You begin to know *Jesus himself* better. You begin to see him more clearly. You begin to understand that everything the Bible teaches about Mary is really based on what it teaches about Christ. That, at least, is what Christians have believed since ancient times. And that is what I've tried to show over and over again in this book.

When you behold Mary as the new Eve, it does not take anything away from Jesus. Instead, it helps you to see more clearly that he is the new Adam, who comes to triumph over sin and death and usher in the new heavens and new earth.

When you behold Mary as the new Ark, it no more takes away from the glory of Christ than the Ark of the Covenant took away from the glory of God. Instead, you come to realize that Jesus is the new Bread of Life, who came down from heaven and was hidden inside the new Ark. He is also the new Moses, who has come to lead us on a journey that begins in this world and will end in the new promised land of the world to come.

When you behold Mary as the queen mother of the kingdom of God, it does not take away anything from the majesty of Jesus the King. To the contrary, you discover that her queenship and virginal motherhood reveal the deepest of all mysteries: that Jesus is truly Immanuel, "God with us."

When you behold Mary as the mysterious mother of the Messiah, you begin to grasp the awesome and terrible truth that Jesus brings salvation *through* suffering and sorrow— not apart from it. And you also begin to realize that these sufferings, however painful, are nothing more than the "birth pangs" of the resurrection from the dead.

When you behold Mary as the new Rachel, mother of the new Joseph, who—against all odds—becomes the savior of the whole world, then you begin to realize that we are beloved younger brothers and sisters. You begin to see that he loves us so much that he even gave us *his* mother to be *our* mother—a mother who knows our sufferings and prays for us, just as Rachel did for her children on earth.

Finally, when you begin to behold Mary and take her to be your own mother, you will discover something amazing and precious. You will discover that *she is already there*, waiting for you. You will discover that Mary was beholding you long before you ever looked at her. You will discover that Mary was praying for you long before you ever began to talk with her. You will find that Mary was loving you long before you ever learned to love her. Because that's how it is with mothers. When a mother gives birth, she sees her child long before the child can even open its eyes to see her. Perhaps that is one reason why Jesus speaks first to Mary: "'Woman, behold, your son!'" (John 19:26). Mary too beholds the Beloved Disciple before he beholds her.

The same thing is true today. Mary, like Jesus himself,

is not dead. She is very much alive in the heavenly kingdom. She already tastes the glory of the resurrection and the new creation. And she is beholding you; she is praying for you; she is loving you. Right now, she is waiting to see if you too will respond to Jesus' last words and take her to be your own: "Behold, *your* mother."

JEWISH SOURCES OUTSIDE THE BIBLE

◇◇◇◇◇

In order to situate the words and deeds of Jesus in their historical context, we need to be familiar with two important sources of information: (1) the Jewish Scriptures, commonly known as the Old Testament, and (2) ancient Jewish tradition, enshrined in a host of writings not contained in the Hebrew Bible and often not familiar to non-Jewish readers who are not already specialists in biblical studies.[1]

For this reason, it is helpful to briefly identify the various collections of Jewish writings outside the Bible that I refer to from time to time in this book. I cannot overemphasize that I am not suggesting that Jesus himself (or even the writers of the New Testament) would have *read* any of these works, some of which were compiled long after his earthly life. What I am suggesting is that many of these writings bear witness to ancient Jewish *traditions* outside the Bible that may have circulated at the time of Jesus. In particular, there are Jewish phrases, customs, practices, and beliefs reflected in both the New Testament and these extrabiblical Jewish writings.

In light of this situation, contemporary scholars such as Dale Allison, Craig Evans, Amy-Jill Levine, Craig Keener, John Meier, E. P. Sanders, Geza Vermes, and many others make abundant use of extrabiblical Jewish sources in their study of the New Testament. For a recent example, see especially *The Jewish Annotated New Testament* (2nd ed.; eds. Amy-Jill Levine and Marc Zvi Brettler; Oxford: Oxford University Press, 2017). In this volume, an international team of Jewish scholars utilizes both Jewish Scripture and extrabiblical writings, including rabbinic literature, to shed light on the meaning of the New Testament.

With this in mind, after the Bible itself, the most important Jewish sources utilized by contemporary scholars are the following:

- *The Dead Sea Scrolls:* an ancient collection of Jewish manuscripts copied sometime between the second century B.C. and 70 A.D. This collection contains numerous writings from the Second Temple Period, during which Jesus lived.

- *The Old Testament Pseudepigrapha:* a vast array of writings that are often attributed to ancient authors such as Enoch, Ezra, Baruch, and others. They span the centuries before and after the time of Jesus (from the second century B.C. through the fourth century A.D.). Many of these works, such as 1 Enoch, Jubilees, 4 Ezra, and 2 Baruch, give key insights into Judaism at the time of Jesus.

- *The Works of Josephus:* the writings of a Jewish historian and Pharisee who lived in the first century A.D. His works are extremely important witnesses to Jewish history and culture at the time of Jesus and the early Church.

- *The Mishnah* and *Tosefta:* two extensive collections of the oral traditions of Jewish rabbis who lived from about 50 B.C. to A.D. 200. Most of the traditions are focused on legal and liturgical matters. For rabbinic Judaism, after the Bible, the Mishnah remains the most authoritative witness to Jewish tradition.

- *The Targums:* ancient Jewish translations and paraphrases of books of the Jewish Scriptures from Hebrew into Aramaic. The Targums emerged sometime after the Babylonian exile (587 B.C.), when many Jews began speaking Aramaic instead of Hebrew. Scholars disagree about their exact dates, which are very difficult to determine.

- *The Babylonian Talmud:* a vast compilation— more than thirty massive volumes—of the traditions of Jewish rabbis who lived from around

A.D. 220 to 500. The Talmud consists of both legal opinions and biblical interpretation, in the form of an extensive commentary on the Mishnah.

- *The Midrash Rabbah:* These texts are ancient Jewish commentaries on various books of the Bible. Although parts of these are later than the Talmud, they contain many interpretations of Scripture attributed to rabbis who lived during the times of the Mishnah and the Talmud.

These are by no means all of the ancient Jewish writings scholars use to understand the New Testament, but they are the ones I have engaged from time to time in this book.

Acknowledgments

◇◇◇◇◇

For years, I've wanted to write a book on the Jewish roots of Mary, but I never felt like I was ready. I kept putting it off, until my dear friend Sr. Julia Darrenkamp, F.S.P., finally twisted my arm—I mean, encouraged me—to just *do* it. So first thanks must go to Sr. Julia, without whom this book would not exist. Thank you especially for your prayers, and for being my sister.

Next in line is my amazing editor at Image Books, Gary Jansen. Words cannot express how much your friendship, support, and guidance over the course of this project have meant to me. Thanks for using your many talents to help me be a better writer. I also want to offer a heartfelt thank-you to all of my friends and colleagues who read and critiqued various drafts of the book: Michael Barber, Todd Russell, Jimmy Seghers, John Sehorn, Edward Sri, and Matt Ziifle. I'm grateful to Jennifer Ely for her positive feedback and for formatting the charts! I'm indebted to Mario Sacasa for patiently listening to me rattle on about Mary and for the breakthrough insight I needed to finish one particularly difficult chapter. I especially want to thank Kevin Redmann, whose truly amazing gift for languages ancient and modern caught countless mistakes I had made. Kevin, you have made this an incalculably better book. As always, I'm grateful to any and all of my friends—clergy, religious, and laity—who have prayed for me and supported me in various ways while I was writing this book, especially Carol and Herb Younger.

In closing, I want to thank my mother, who first introduced me to Jesus and to his mother. My image of Mary will always be shaped by you. Then, of course, there is my beautiful wife, Elizabeth, and our children: Morgen, Aidan, Hannah, Marybeth, and Lillia. Elizabeth, you alone know the sacrifices and suffering that went into the writing of this particular book. May they be for the greater glory of God. In a special way, this book is dedicated to Aidan, my son. May you always listen to the last words Mary speaks in the Gospel: "Do whatever he tells you" (John 2:5).

MAY 21, 2018

MEMORIAL OF MARY, MOTHER OF THE CHURCH

Notes

◇◇◇◇◇

Epigraph

1. Jacob of Serug, *On the Mother of God* (trans. Mary Hansbury; Crestwood, NY: St. Vladimir's Seminary Press, 1998), 20–21.

Chapter 1: Introduction

1. See *The Scriptural Rosary* (ill. V. Broderick; Glenview: Christianica, 1966).

2. For the story of Elizabeth's grandparents, see John Caylor, *In Evangeline's Country: A Study of Baptist Missions Among the French* (Atlanta: Home Mission Board, 1954), 59–71.

3. Brant Pitre, *Jesus and the Jewish Roots of the Eucharist* (New York: Image, 2011).

4. Unless otherwise noted, all Scripture quotations are from the *Revised Standard Version, Catholic Edition* (Toronto: Thomas Nelson & Sons, 1966). All emphasis in Scripture quotations is the author's. For a recent study of the pagan "queen of heaven" in ancient Israel, see Susan Ackerman, "'And the Women Knead Dough': The Worship of the Queen of Heaven in Sixth-Century Judah," in *Women in the Hebrew Bible: A Reader* (ed. Alice Bach; New York and London: Routledge, 1999), 21–32.

5. See especially Scott Hahn, *Hail, Holy Queen: The Mother of God in the Word of God* (New York: Doubleday, 2001). For other recent studies, see

Gary Anderson, "Mary in the Old Testament," *Pro Ecclesia* 16 (2007): 33–55; and P. Ladouceur, "Old Testament Prefigurations of the Mother of God," *St. Vladimir's Theological Quarterly* 50 (2006): 5–57.

6. For surveys of ancient Christian beliefs about Mary, see especially Brian K. Reynolds, *Gateway to Heaven: Marian Doctrine and Devotion, Image and Typology in the Patristic and Medieval Periods* (2 vols.; Hyde Park: New City Press, 2012); Luigi Gambero, *Mary and the Fathers of the Church: The Blessed Virgin Mary in Patristic Thought* (trans. Thomas Buffer; San Francisco: Ignatius, 1999); Jaroslav Pelikan, *Mary through the Centuries: Her Place in the History of Culture* (New Haven: Yale University Press, 1996); Michael O'Carroll, C.S.Sp., *Theotokos: A Theological Encyclopedia of the Blessed Virgin Mary* (repr.; Eugene, OR: Wipf & Stock, 2000 [orig. 1982]).

7. *Catechism of the Catholic Church* (2nd ed.; Washington, DC: United States Conference of Catholic Bishops, 1997) (emphasis added). See also Pelikan, *Mary Through the Centuries*, 75: "[F]or Christian orthodoxy ... the key to the correct understanding both of who Jesus was and of what he did was Mary, his mother."

8. Joseph Cardinal Ratzinger, *Daughter Zion: Meditations on the Church's Marian Belief* (trans. John M. McDermott, S.J.; San Francisco: Ignatius, 1983), 12.

9. Timothy George, "The Blessed Virgin Mary in Evangelical Perspective," in *Mary: Mother of God* (eds. Carl E. Braaten and Robert W. Jenson; Grand Rapids: Eerdmans, 2004), 106 (emphasis added). For an Eastern Orthodox perspective on the importance of typology for understanding Mary, see Mary B. Cunningham, *Gateway to Life: Orthodox Thinking on the Mother of God* (Yonkers, NY: St. Vladimir's Seminary Press, 2015), 27; and *The Orthodox Study Bible* (ed. Jack Norman Sparks et al.; Nashville: Thomas Nelson, 2008), 1228.

10. See, for example, the otherwise thorough study by Tim Perry, *Mary for Evangelicals: Toward an Understanding of the Mother of Our Lord* (Downers Grove, IL: IVP Academic, 2006), 19–115. Perry's treatment of Mary in the New Testament consistently ignores the biblical parallels between Mary and Eve, the Ark, the queen mother, et cetera.

11. In the words of one prominent evangelical New Testament scholar: "We are Protestants; we believe in the Bible; Mary is in the Bible; we need to believe what the Bible says about Mary." Scot McKnight, *The Real Mary: Why Evangelical Christians Can Embrace the Mother of Jesus* (Brewster, MA: Paraclete, 2007), 5.

Chapter 2: The New Eve

1. See Craig A. Evans and L. Novakovic, "Typology," in *Dictionary of Jesus and the Gospels* (eds. Joel B. Green, Jeannine K. Brown, and Nicholas

Perrin; Downers Grove, IL: IVP Academic, 2013), 988; G. K. Beale, *A New Testament Biblical Theology: The Unfolding of the Old Testament in the New* (Grand Rapids: Baker Academic, 2011), 381–429; Joachim Jeremias, "Adam," in *Theological Dictionary of the New Testament* (10 vols.; eds. Gerhard Kittel et al.; trans. Geoffrey W. Bromiley; Grand Rapids: Eerdmans, 1964), 1:141–43.

2. See Thomas D. Stegman, S.J., "Paul's Use of *DIKAIO-* Terminology: Moving Beyond N. T. Wright's Forensic Interpretation," *Theological Studies* 72 (2011): 496–524 (esp. 519).

3. See Carol Meyers, "Eve," in *Women in Scripture: A Dictionary of Named and Unnamed Women in the Hebrew Bible, the Apocryphal/Deuterocanonical Books, and the New Testament* (eds. Carol Meyers, Toni Craven, and Ross S. Kraemer; Grand Rapids: Eerdmans, 2001), 79–82; Howard N. Wallace, "Eve," in *Anchor Bible Dictionary* (ed. David Noel Freedman; 6 vols.; Anchor Bible Reference Library; New York: Doubleday, 1992), 2:676–77.

4. Claus Westermann, *Genesis 1–11: A Commentary* (trans. John J. Scullion, S.J.; Minneapolis: Fortress, 1984), 166.

5. Umberto Cassuto, *A Commentary on the Book of Genesis: Part I* (trans. Israel Abrahams; Jerusalem: Magness, 1989), 162.

6. RSVCE, slightly adapted.

7. Unfortunately, the RSV leaves out this key Hebrew phrase. It is present in all other major English versions (KJV, NAB, NRSV, etc.).

8. Some readers assume that that the verb "greatly multiply" (Hebrew *harbah arbeh*) (Genesis 3:16 RSV) implies that Eve would have experienced labor pains before the Fall. However popular this view has become in recent years, it is likely incorrect. For one thing, the Hebrew expression puts the emphasis on the multiplicity and intensity of the pains, not on Eve's state prior to the Fall. The Jewish Publication Society translation does a good job of capturing the sense of the text: "I will *make most severe* your pangs in childbearing" (Genesis 3:16 JPS). Moreover, in keeping with Genesis' love for plays on words, the Hebrew word "multiply" (Hebrew *rabah*) is likely chosen because it echoes God's first command to Adam and Eve: "Be fruitful and *multiply* (Hebrew *rebu*)" (Genesis 1:28). Whereas Adam and Eve were supposed to "multiply" their offspring, because of sin, God now "multiplies" Eve's suffering. In choosing this word, the author of Genesis no more implies that Eve had birth pangs before the Fall than that Adam experienced fruitless toil or death before he sinned. Finally, ancient Jewish and Christian interpreters did not read Genesis 3:16 as implying pain in childbirth before the Fall. For example, Josephus explicitly states that God "punished" Eve by the "birth-pangs" (Greek *ōdinōn*) that come with "childbirth" (Greek *toketois*) (Josephus, *Antiquities*, 1.48–49). As we will see in Chapter 5, ancient Christian writers will also unanimously consider the pains of

childbirth to be the result of the first sin. In the words of the contemporary Jewish commentator Nahum Sarna: "Intense pain in childbearing is unique to the human species and generally unknown to other female mammals. It therefore calls for explanation . . . [T]he rigors of childbearing are presented here [in Genesis 3:16] as a *consequence* of partaking of the tree of knowledge." Nahum Sarna, *Genesis* (JPS Torah Commentary; Philadelphia: Jewish Publication Society, 1989), 27–28 (emphasis added).

9. I have altered the Revised Standard Version's "bruise" to "strike" (Hebrew *suph*), since "strike" is a better translation of the original Hebrew. See Victor Hamilton, *Genesis* (2 vols.; New International Commentary on the Old Testament; Grand Rapids: Eerdmans, 1990, 1995), 1:198; Westermann, *Genesis 1–11*, 260.

10. NRSV; see Hamilton, *Genesis*, 1.197–99; Westermann, *Genesis 1–11*, 259–61.

11. For Eve in Jewish tradition, see Alice Ogden Bellis, "Eve in the Apocryphal/Deuterocanonical Books," in *Women in Scripture: A Dictionary of Named and Unnamed Women in the Hebrew Bible, the Apocryphal/Deuterocanonical Books, and the New Testament* (eds. Carol Meyers, Toni Craven, and Ross S. Kraemer; Grand Rapids: Eerdmans, 2001), 82–83; James L. Kugel, *Traditions of the Bible: A Guide to the Bible as It Was at the Start of the Common Era* (Cambridge: Harvard University Press, 1998), 94–144.

12. Kugel, *Traditions of the Bible*, 96–97.

13. James H. Charlesworth, ed., *The Old Testament Pseudepigrapha* (2 vols.; Anchor Bible Reference Library; New York: Doubleday, 1983, 1985), 2.279 (hereafter cited as Charlesworth, *OTP*).

14. Kugel, *Traditions of the Bible*, 100–103.

15. Charlesworth, *OTP*, 2.322.

16. Charlesworth, *OTP*, 1.541.

17. See Kugel, *Traditions of the Bible*, 130. On the doctrine of original sin, see *Catechism of the Catholic Church*, nos. 404–5.

18. Charlesworth, *OTP*, 1:43. I am here following Ephraim Isaac's own literal translation (in Charlesworth, *OTP*, 1.43, n. j). See also George W. E. Nickelsburg and James C. VanderKam, *1 Enoch 2* (Hermeneia; Minneapolis: Fortress, 2012), 114, who also clarify that the Ethiopic means "'the son of the progeny of the mother of the living,' that is, Eve."

19. Martin McNamara, M.S.C., *Targum Neofiti 1: Genesis* (Aramaic Bible 1A; Collegeville: Liturgical Press, 1992), 61.

20. Some scholars date it as late as the 3rd or 4th century A.D. See Martin McNamara, *Targum and Testament Revisited: Aramaic Paraphrases of the Hebrew Bible* (2nd ed.; Grand Rapids: Eerdmans, 2010), 129–40.

21. See Kugel, *Traditions of the Bible*, 99–100; Joseph Klausner, *The Messianic Idea in Israel: From Its Beginning to the Completion of the Mishnah* (trans. W. F. Winespring; London: George Allen & Unwin, 1956), 26.

22. RSVCE, slightly adapted.

23. See Richard Bauckham, *Gospel of Glory: Major Themes in Johannine Theology* (Grand Rapids: Baker Academic, 2015), 132–35; Francis Martin and William M. Wright IV, *The Gospel of John* (Grand Rapids: Baker Academic, 2015), 42–61; John F. McHugh, *John 1–4* (International Critical Commentary; London: Bloomsbury T. & T. Clark, 2014), 176–77.

24. Beverly Gaventa, *Mary: Glimpses of the Mother of Jesus* (Minneapolis: Fortress, 1999), 85. So too McKnight, *The Real Mary*, 66: "For Jesus to have used the word *woman* for his mother at the Wedding at Cana was neither impolite nor rude."

25. Raymond E. Brown, *The Gospel according to John* (2 vols.; Anchor Bible 29–29A; New York: Doubleday, 1965, 1970), 1:109 (slightly adapted; emphasis added).

26. See Genesis 2:22, 23; 3:1, 2, 4, 6, 12, 13 (2x), 15, 16.

27. John Dominic Crossan, *The Gospel of Eternal Life: Reflections on the Theology of St. John* (Milwaukee: The Bruce, 1967), 57 (emphasis added). So too Brown, *The Gospel according to John*, 2:926: "Jesus' mother is the New Eve."

28. For discussion, see Craig R. Koester, *Revelation* (Anchor Yale Bible 38A; New Haven: Yale University Press, 2014), 523–67; G. K. Beale, *The Book of Revelation* (The New International Greek Testament Commentary; Grand Rapids: Eerdmans, 1999), 621–32; David E. Aune, *Revelation* (3 vols.; Word Biblical Commentary 52–52C; Nashville: Thomas Nelson, 1998), 2:647–713. Although dated, the full-length study of Bernard J. Le Frois, *The Woman Clothed with the Sun (Ap. 12): Individual or Collective? An Exegetical Study* (Rome: Orbis Catholicus, 1954), remains unsurpassed.

29. See LeFrois, *Woman*, 38–58.

30. See LeFrois, *Woman*, 11–38.

31. See Koester, *Revelation*, 546, 549–50; Beale, *The Book of Revelation*, 633–34; 639–40; Aune, *Revelation*, 2:683–84, 689.

32. See Aune, *Revelation*, 2:683–84; Beale, *The Book of Revelation*, 633.

33. Koester, *Revelation*, 543.

34. Ben Witherington III, *What Have They Done with Jesus? Beyond Strange Theories and Bad History—Why We Can Trust the Bible* (San Francisco: HarperOne, 2006), 130.

35. McKnight, *The Real Mary*, 120. For a Jewish scholar who comes to the same conclusion, see David Flusser, Jaroslav Pelikan, and Justin Lang, O.F.M., *Mary: Images of the Mother of Jesus in Jewish and Christian Perspective* (Philadephia: Fortress, 1986), 16: "Christian theologians and thinkers were justified in interpreting the woman of the twelfth chapter of Revelation as Mary."

36. For identifications of the woman in Revelation 12 as Mary, see Ephraim the Syrian, *Hymns on the Nativity*, 4; Epiphanius of Salamis, *Panarion* 78.11, 3–4. Translations in Philip Schaff, ed., *Nicene and Post-Nicene Fathers, Second Series* (14 vols.; repr.; Peabody, MA: Hendrickson, 1994), 13:236 (hereafter cited as Schaff, *NPNF2*); Frank Williams, ed., *The Panarion of Epiphanius of Salamis* (2 vols.; Nag Hammadi and Manichean Studies; Leiden: Brill; Atlanta: Society of Biblical Literature, 2009, 2013), 2:624–25. For the identification of the woman in Revelation 12 as the Church, see Methodius of Olympus, *The Banquet of the Ten Virgins*, 8.5–6. Translation in Alexander Roberts and James Donaldson, eds., *Ante-Nicene Fathers* (12 vols.; repr.; Peabody, MA: Hendrickson, 1994), 6:336–37 (hereafter cited as Roberts and Donaldson, *ANF*).

37. For the Catholic doctrine of the immaculate conception, see *Catechism of the Catholic Church*, nos. 490–92. I will not attempt here to trace out the historical development of the doctrine. I simply want to show its (often ignored) biblical roots in the New Testament portrait of Mary and Eve. For studies of its development, see Reynolds, *Gateway to Heaven*, 330–69; Sarah Jane Boss, "The Development of the Doctrine of Mary's Immaculate Conception," in *Mary: The Complete Resource* (ed. Sarah Jane Boss; Oxford and New York: Oxford University Press, 2007), 207–35.

38. See Gary A. Anderson, *The Genesis of Perfection: Adam and Eve in Jewish and Christian Imagination* (Louisville: Westminster John Knox, 2001), 43–62.

39. Roberts and Donaldson, *ANF*, 1:249.

40. Roberts and Donaldson, *ANF*, 1:455.

41. Schaff, *NPNF2*, 13:254.

42. Translation in Gambero, *Mary and the Fathers of the Church*, 135. See also Schaff, *NPNF2*, 7:75.

43. St. John Chrysostom, *Commentary on the Psalms* (2 vols.; trans. Robert Charles Hill; Brookline, MA: Holy Cross Orthodox Press, 1998), 1:271.

44. Schaff, *NPNF2*, 6:30.

45. Translation in Gambero, *Mary and the Fathers of the Church*, 230.

46. See Philip Boyce, ed., *Mary: The Virgin Mary in the Life and Writings of John Henry Newman* (Leominster: Gracewing; Grand Rapids: Eerdmans, 1999), 206. See also John Henry Newman, *An Essay on the Development of Christian Doctrine* (Notre Dame, IN: University of Notre Dame Press, 1989), 415–18.

47. See Reynolds, *Gateway to Heaven*, 330–48.

48. Translation in Gambero, *Mary and the Fathers of the Church*, 109.

49. Translation in Philip Schaff, ed., *Nicene and Post-Nicene Fathers, First Series* (14 vols.; repr.; Peabody, MA: Hendrickson, 1994), 5:135 (hereafter cited as Schaff, *NPNF1*).

50. Cf. Mary Cunningham, *Gateway of Life*, 182–84, who writes that Ortho-

dox churches object to the Catholic doctrine of the immaculate conception because it results in Mary's "separation from the rest of humanity,"
makes her "physical nature in some way different from that of all other
mortals," and removes Mary's "freedom of choice." However, in Scripture, Adam and Eve are created without sin and yet are both fully human
and truly free. In a similar way, according to Catholic teaching, the conception of Mary without sin *in no way* takes away from her freedom or
her fully human nature. See *Catechism of the Catholic Church*, nos. 374–
79. Compare McKnight, *The Real Mary*, 121, who rightly notes that for
Catholics, "Mary's sinlessness was not because she was divine. Mary's
sinlessness in official teaching is solely the product of God's grace."

51. On this point, see especially the words of John Henry Newman: "If Eve
     had this supernatural inward gift given her from the first moment of
     her personal existence, is it possible to deny that Mary too had this gift
     from the very first moment of her personal existence? I do not know
     how to resist this inference—well, this is simply and literally the doc-
     trine of the Immaculate Conception. I say that the doctrine of the Im-
     maculate Conception is in its substance this, and nothing more or less
     than this . . . and it really does seem to me bound up in the doctrine of
     the Fathers, that Mary is the second Eve." Quoted in Boyce, *Mary*, 225.
     For the original letter to Reverend Pusey, see John Henry Newman,
     Certain Difficulties Felt by Anglicans in Catholic Teaching (2 vols.; London:
     1908, 1910), 2:44–50.

52. See McKnight, *The Real Mary*, 130–31, for the erroneous claim that
     "the doctrine of the immaculate conception" is meant to explain how
     Mary does not "pass on her sinful nature to Jesus." It is significant that
     McKnight does not actually cite Catholic teaching (such as the *Cat-
     echism of the Catholic Church*) in support of this explanation, for no such
     teaching exists.

53. This line is cited in *Catechism of the Catholic Church*, no. 419. For the full
     context, see Pius IX, Apostolic Constitution Defining the Dogma of the
     Immaculate Conception, *Ineffabilis Deus* (Boston: Pauline Books, n.d.
     [originally issued December 8, 1854]), 21.

54. For more on the new Eve and the immaculate conception, see John
     Paul II, *Theotókos: Woman, Disciple, Mother—A Catechesis on Mary the
     Mother of God* (Boston: Pauline Books, 2000), 90–107; Denis Farkas-
     falvy, O.Cist., *The Marian Mystery: Outline of a Mariology* (Staten Island;
     Alba House, 2014), 282–90; Aidan Nichols, O.P., *There Is No Rose: The
     Mariology of the Catholic Church* (Minneapolis: Fortress, 2017), 45–66.

Chapter 3: The New Ark

1.   See C. L. Seow, "Ark of the Covenant," in *Anchor Bible Dictionary* (ed.
     David Noel Freedman; 6 vols.; Anchor Bible Reference Library; New

York: Doubleday, 1992), 1:386–93; Roland de Vaux, *Ancient Israel: Its Life and Institutions* (trans. John McHugh; repr.; Grand Rapids: Eerdmans, 1997 [orig. 1961]), 297–302.

2. For an in-depth discussion of the Ark (with illustrations), see William H. C. Propp, *Exodus* (Anchor Bible 2–2A; New York: Doubleday, 1999, 2006), 2:372–92. See also Victor H. Hamilton, *Exodus: An Exegetical Commentary* (Grand Rapids: Baker Academic, 2011), 454–60.

3. Propp, *Exodus*, 2:376: the Ark is the place of "theophany."

4. According to the Old Testament, by the time King Solomon built the Temple, almost five centuries after the exodus, two of the three items were missing (see 1 Kings 8:9). No explanation is given for how the manna and the rod went missing.

5. Hamilton, *Exodus*, 455; Irene Jacob and Walter Jacob, "Flora," in *Anchor Bible Dictionary* (ed. David Noel Freedman; 6 vols.; Anchor Bible Reference Library; New York: Doubleday, 1992), 2:804.

6. Greek *xyla asēpta*. Note: LXX (Roman numeral seventy) indicates a quotation from the Greek translation of the Jewish Scriptures known as the "Septuagint" (from the Latin for "seventy"). See Propp, *Exodus*, 2:375; L. C. L. Brenton, *The Septuagint with Apocrypha: Greek and English* (repr.; Peabody, MA: Hendrickson, 1986), 102: "incorruptible wood."

7. William Whiston, *The Works of Josephus: Complete and Unabridged* (new ed.; Peabody, MA: Hendrickson, 1987), 87.

8. Cf. Genesis 8:20; Psalm 51:12; Francis Brown, S. R. Driver, and Charles A. Briggs, *A Hebrew and English Lexicon of the Old Testament* (Oxford: Oxford University Press, 1952), 373.

9. Propp, *Exodus*, 2:380.

10. Propp, *Exodus*, 2:673.

11. See Seow, "Ark of the Covenant," 389–90.

12. See Seow, "Ark of the Covenant," 391; Delbert R. Hillers, "Ritual Procession of the Ark and Psalm 132," *Catholic Biblical Quarterly* 30 (1968): 48–55.

13. See John Goldingay, *Psalms* (3 vols.; Baker Commentary on the Old Testament Wisdom and Psalms; Grand Rapids: Baker Academic, 2008), 2:545, 752.

14. RSVCE, slightly adapted. (For the sake of clarity, I have adapted the archaic use of "thee" and "thou" here).

15. Mordechai Cogan, *1 Kings* (Anchor Bible 10; New York: Doubleday, 2001), 280–81.

16. See I. Kalimi and J. D. Purvis, "The Hiding of the Temple Vessels in Jewish and Samaritan Literature," *Catholic Biblical Quarterly* 56 (1994): 679–85; Menahem Haran, "The Disappearance of the Ark," *Israel Exploration Journal* 13 (1963): 46–58.

17. See Robert Doran, "The Second Book of Maccabees," in *The New Interpreter's Bible, Volume IV* (Nashville: Abingdon, 1996), 198. It is worth noting that the ancient Jewish writer Eupolemus (2nd century B.C.) corroborates the tradition that Jeremiah saved the Ark. See Eusebius, *The Preparation for the Gospel*, 9.39.5.

18. Whiston, *The Works of Josephus*, 707.

19. *Tacitus: Histories, Books IV–V, Annals Books I–III* (trans. Clifford H. Moore and John Jackson; Loeb Classical Library 249; Cambridge: Harvard University Press, 1925), 191.

20. See Amy-Jill Levine, "Luke," in *The Jewish Annotated New Testament* (2nd ed.; eds. Amy-Jill Levine and Marc Zvi Brettler; Oxford: Oxford University Press, 2017), 111, n. 35; 110, n. 15; Frederick William Danker, *A Greek-English Lexicon of the New Testament and Other Early Christian Literature* (3rd ed.; Chicago and London: University of Chicago Press, 2000), 378–79; Luke Timothy Johnson, *The Gospel of Luke* (Sacra Pagina 3; Collegeville: Liturgical Press, 1991), 38. See especially John McHugh, *The Mother of Jesus in the New Testament* (London: Darton, Longman & Todd, 1975), 58: "Likewise, St Luke, when he wrote the word 'overshadow,' must have known what associations it would evoke in the Jewish mind. No Jew, reading the words, 'A Power of the Most High will overshadow thee,' could fail to think of the Divine Presence or Shekinah."

21. John Nolland, *Luke* (2 vols.; Word Biblical Commentary 35A–35B; Dallas: Word Books, 1989, 1993), 1:54.

22. For example, the parallels between Mary and the Ark receive no discussion in John T. Carroll, *Luke* (New Testament Library; Louisville: Westminster John Knox, 2012); McKnight, *The Real Mary*; Perry, *Mary for Evangelicals*; Amy-Jill Levine with Maria Mayo Robbins, eds., *A Feminist Companion to Mariology* (London: T. & T. Clark, 2005); Carl E. Braaten and Robert W. Jensen, eds., *Mary, Mother of God* (Grand Rapids: Eerdmans, 2004); Beverly Roberts Gaventa and Cynthia L. Rigby, eds., *Blessed One: Protestant Perspectives on Mary* (Louisville: Westminster John Knox, 2002); François Bovon, *Luke* (3 vols.; Hermeneia; Minneapolis: Fortress, 2002, 2012, 2013); Gaventa, *Mary: Glimpses of the Mother of Jesus*.

23. See, for example, the ecumenically coauthored book, *Mary in the New Testament* (eds. Raymond E. Brown, Karl P. Donfried, Joseph A. Fitzmyer, and John Reumann; Minneapolis: Fortress; Mahwah: Paulist, 1978), 132–34. After listing the parallels between Mary in Luke and the Ark in Exodus 40 and 2 Samuel 6, this team of scholars dismisses them using remarkably weak arguments. For example, they contend that the identification of Mary with the Ark hangs on a "facile combination of Luke 1:32–33, 35 and John 1:14" (ibid., 134). This is simply false. The five verbal parallels between the Ark and Mary in Luke's Gospel

stand on their own and demand some plausible explanation for their existence. Unfortunately, the authors of *Mary in the New Testament* never provide any.

24. See, for example, David W. Pao and Eckhard Schnabel, "Luke," in *Commentary on the New Testament Use of the Old Testament* (eds. G. K. Beale and D. A. Carson; Grand Rapids: Baker Academic, 2007), 260–61; Darrell L. Bock, *Luke* (2 vols.; Baker Exegetical Commentary on the New Testament; Grand Rapids: Baker Academic, 1994, 1996), 1:137; Joseph A. Fitzmyer, *The Gospel according to Luke* (2 vols.; Anchor Bible 28–28A; New York: Doubleday, 1983, 1985), 1:364. In the words of Raymond Brown, *The Birth of the Messiah* (rev. ed.; Anchor Bible Reference Library; New York: Doubleday, 1993), 328, "the evidence" for Mary as the new Ark in Luke 1–2 "is *cumulative.*" It is not based on the presence of a single parallel, but of the striking fact of some five parallels with the Ark in Jewish Scripture. Unfortunately, Brown himself never responds to the force of the cumulative argument.

25. So Sarah Jane Boss, *Mary: The Complete Resource* (ed. Sarah Jane Boss; Oxford and New York: Oxford University Press, 2007), 2: "Luke presents Mary as the Ark, as we can see from the parallel that he draws with the narrative of King David taking the Ark to Jerusalem in 2 Samuel 6." See also André Feuillet, *Jesus and His Mother: According to the Lucan Infancy Narratives, and According to St. John* (trans. Leonard Maluf; Still River, MA: St. Bede's, 1984), 12–13. As far as I can tell, the first contemporary biblical scholar to recognize the presence of these parallels between Mary and the Ark in Luke was the early twentieth-century Jesuit archaeologist (and friend of Dame Agatha Christie), Eric Burrows, S.J., *The Gospel of the Infancy* (ed. E. F. Sutcliffe; London: Burns, Oates & Washbourne, 1940), 47–49, 56, n. 1.

26. Max Thurian, *Mary, Mother of All Christians* (trans. Neville B. Cryer; New York: Herder & Herder, 1964), 49, 51.

27. Burrows, *The Gospel of the Infancy*, 48.

28. RSV (slightly adapted).

29. See Bruce Metzger, *The Early Versions of the New Testament: Their Origin, Transmission, and Limitations* (Oxford: Oxford University Press, 1977), 347.

30. See Koester, *Revelation*, 524–25; Aune, *Revelation*, 2:661–62.

31. Aune, *Revelation*, 2:677.

32. Koester, *Revelation*, 524.

33. O'Carroll, *Theotokos*, 50. See also Burrows, *The Gospel of the Infancy*, 48.

34. Quoted in Theodoret, *Dialogue* 1. See Schaff, *NPNF2*, 3:177 (slightly adapted).

35. Translation in Gambero, *Mary and the Fathers of the Church*, 106.

36. Jacob of Serug, *On the Mother of God*, 74.

37. For the Catholic dogma of the Assumption, see *Catechism of the Catholic Church*, no. 966. See also Joseph Ratzinger and Hans Urs von Balthasar, *Mary: The Church at the Source* (trans. Adrian Walker; repr.; San Francisco: Ignatius, 2005 [orig. 1980]), 65; O'Carroll, *Theotokos*, 50, 55–58.

38. The earliest church father to refer to Mary's being "taken up" into heaven at the end of her life is the fourth-century writer Epiphanius of Salamis, who identified "the woman" of Revelation 12 as "Mary" (Epiphanius, *Panarion*, 79.5,1; 78.11). The sixth-century commentator Oecumenius also identifies "the woman clothed with the sun" in Revelation 12 as "the mother of our Savior" and declares that "the vision describes her as being *in heaven and not on earth*, as pure in soul *and body...*" (Oecumenius, *Commentary on the Apocalypse* (trans. John N. Suggit; *The Fathers of the Church* 112; Washington, DC: Catholic University of America Press, 2006), 6.19.1–2. See Gambero, *Mary and the Fathers of the Church*, 126.

39. See Brian E. Daley, S.J., *On the Dormition of Mary: Early Patristic Homilies* (Popular Patristics 18; Crestwood, NY: St. Vladimir's Seminary Press, 1998), 88. For reasons of space, I have abbreviated the lengthy titles of both encomiums.

40. See Daley, *On the Dormition of Mary*, 204–5.

41. See Pius XII, Apostolic Constitution Defining the Dogma of the Assumption, *Munificentissimus Deus* (Boston: Pauline, n.d.), 12–13. For an Eastern Orthodox perspective on Mary's "Falling Asleep" (Greek *Koimēsis*) and entrance into heaven, see John Anthony McGuckin, *The Orthodox Church: An Introduction to Its History, Doctrine, and Spiritual Culture* (West Sussex: Wiley-Blackwell, 2011), 218–19.

42. Benedict XVI, "Homily Mass for the Solemnity of the Assumption of the Blessed Virgin Mary" (August 15, 2011), available at www.vatican.va.

43. For more on Mary's assumption, see Matthew Levering, *Mary's Bodily Assumption* (Notre Dame: University of Notre Dame Press, 2015); Farkasfalvy, *The Marian Mystery*, 291–97; John Paul II, *Theotókos*, 203–11.

Chapter 4: The Queen Mother

1. See N. T. Wright, *How God Became King: The Forgotten Story of the Gospels* (San Francisco: HarperOne, 2012).

2. For Jesus as a new David, see Y. Miura, "Son of David," in *Dictionary of Jesus and the Gospels* (eds. Joel B. Green, Jeannine K. Brown, and Nicholas Perrin; Downers Grove: IVP Academic, 2013), 881–86; Y. S. Chae, *Jesus as the Eschatological Davidic Shepherd* (Wissenschaftliche Untersuchungen zum Neuen Testament 2.216; Tübingen: Mohr Siebeck, 2006).

3. See Susan Ackerman, "The Queen Mother and the Cult in Ancient Israel," in *Women in the Hebrew Bible: A Reader* (ed. Alice Bach; New York

and London: Routledge, 1999), 179–94; Linda Schearing, "Queen," in *Anchor Bible Dictionary* (6 vols.; ed. David Noel Freedman; New York: Doubleday, 1992), 5:583–88.

4. Schearing, "Queen," 583.

5. Cogan, *1 Kings*, 176–81.

6. De Vaux, *Ancient Israel*, 118.

7. RSVCE, slightly adapted.

8. Cogan, *1 Kings*, 176.

9. De Vaux, *Ancient Israel*, 118. See also Cogan, *1 Kings*, 397, citing 1 Kings 15:13; 2 Chronicles 36:3.

10. Jack R. Lundbom, *Jeremiah* (3 vols.; Anchor Bible 21A–C; New York: Doubleday, 1999, 2004, 2004), 1:681.

11. RSVCE, slightly adapted. The Hebrew is most literally rendered as addressing the King as "God" (Hebrew *'elohim*). See John J. Collins, *The Scepter and the Star: Messianism in Light of the Dead Sea Scrolls* (2nd ed.; Grand Rapids: Eerdmans, 2010), 236.

12. See Goldingay, *Psalms*, 2:60; Christoph Schroeder, "A Love Song," *Catholic Biblical Quarterly* 58 (1996): 417–32 (see 428–29); De Vaux, *Ancient Israel*, 119.

13. Susan Ackerman, *Warrior, Dancer, Seductress, Queen: Women in Judges and Biblical Israel* (Anchor Bible Reference Library; New York: Doubleday, 1998), 137.

14. Schearing, "Queen," 5:586; Ackerman, *Warrior, Dancer, Seductress, Queen*, 137.

15. RSVCE, adapted.

16. For recent discussion, see Adele Berlin and Marc Zvi Brettler, ed., *The Jewish Study Bible* (2nd ed.; Oxford: Oxford University Press, 2014), 780–81; Joseph Blenkinsopp, *Isaiah* (3 vols.; Anchor Bible 19A–19C; New York: Doubleday, 2000, 2003), 1:227–34; Susan Ackerman, "Isa 7:14 Young Woman," in *Women in Scripture: A Dictionary of Named and Unnamed Women in the Hebrew Bible, the Apocryphal/Deuterocanonical Books, and the New Testament* (eds. Carol Meyers, Toni Craven, and Ross S. Kraemer; Grand Rapids: Eerdmans, 2001), 317.

17. RSVCE, slightly adapted (see note 18 below).

18. Francis I. Anderson and David Noel Freedman, *Micah* (Anchor Yale Bible 24E; New Haven: Yale University Press, 2000), 468.

19. I have altered the RSVCE to "until she who bears gives birth" to better reflect the Hebrew expression *yoledah yaladah*, which literally means "until she who bears bears." See Delbert R. Hillers, *Micah* (Hermeneia; Philadelphia: Fortress, 1984), 64.

20. Anderson and Freedman, *Micah*, 469.

NOTES

21. See Hans Walter Wolff, *Micah: A Commentary* (trans. Gary Stansell; Minneapolis: Fortress, 1990), 145: the passage is "best explained if we see in [Mic 5] v. 2 an allusion to Isa. 7:14." Consider the following parallels:

Mother of Immanuel	Mother of the Messiah
Therefore he will give …	Therefore he will give …
and she will give birth	and she will give birth …
and shall call his name Immanuel	the ruler born in Bethlehem.
(Isaiah 7:14)	(Micah 5:3, 2)

22. See especially Edward Sri, *Queen Mother: A Biblical Theology of Mary's Queenship* (Steubenville: Emmaus Academic, 2005). Sri's study is easily the most thorough and best treatment of the queen mother in the New Testament to date.

23. See Susan Ackerman, "The Queen Mother and the Cult in the Ancient Near East," in *Women and Goddess Traditions in Antiquity and Today* (ed. Karen L. King; Minneapolis: Fortress, 1997), 196: "If Jesus is characterized as the royal Messiah, Israel's new king, then Mary, at least figuratively, is depicted as queen mother." See also Sri, *Queen Mother*, 67–78; Brown, *The Birth of the Messiah*, 192, n. 32.

24. See Schearing, "Queen," 585; Brown, *The Birth of the Messiah*, 192, n. 32.

25. See Ackerman, "The Queen Mother and the Cult in the Ancient Near East," 197.

26. For discussion, see Brown, *The Birth of the Messiah*, 122–64; W. D. Davies and Dale C. Allison, Jr., *Matthew* (3 vols.; International Critical Commentary; London: T. & T. Clark, 1988, 1991, 1997), 1:213–27; McHugh, *The Mother of Jesus in the New Testament*, 269–77.

27. Ulrich Luz, *Matthew: A Commentary* (3 vols.; trans. James E. Crouch; Hermeneia; Minneapolis: Fortress, 2007, 2001, 2005), 1:97; Craig S. Keener, *Matthew: A Socio-Rhetorical Commentary* (Grand Rapids: Eerdmans, 2009), 90; Brown, *The Birth of the Messiah*, 132.

28. See Brown, *The Birth of the Messiah*, 344. For Psalm 110:1 in the Greek Septuagint, see Psalm 109:1 (LXX).

29. Sri, *Queen Mother*, 87. See also Feuillet, *Jesus and His Mother*, 13: "The dignity recognized in Mary by Elizabeth in greeting her as she did could thus be related to the authority which in ancient Israel was attributed to the Queen-mother or *gebirah* …"

30. See Levine, "Luke," 111 note on Luke 1:43. For divine implications of "Lord" in Luke 1:43, see also Richard Hays, *Echoes of Scripture in the Gospels* (Waco: Baylor University Press, 2016), 253; C. Kavin Rowe, *Early Narrative Christology: The Lord in the Gospel of Luke* (Grand Rapids: Baker Academic, 2006), 45.

31. McHugh, *The Mother of Jesus in the New Testament*, 74, 76.

32. Cf. Bovon, *Luke*, 1:62; Brown, *The Birth of the Messiah*, 337.

33. Intriguingly, Psalm 45 was later interpreted by ancient Jews as a prophecy of the Messiah. See H. Ausloos, "Psalm 45, Messianic, and the Septuagint," in *The Septuagint and Messianism* (ed. M. A. Knibb; Leuven: Leuven University Press, 2006), 239–51.

34. See Sri, *Queen Mother*, 99, n. 183; Le Frois, *The Woman Clothed with the Sun*, 207–62, for an extensive list of ancient and modern interpreters who identify the woman in Revelation 12 as Mary.

35. See Koester, *Revelation*, 543; Beale, *The Book of Revelation*, 625.

36. Beale, *The Book of Revelation*, 627.

37. Beale, *The Book of Revelation*, 631–32.

38. Aune, *Revelation*, 2.713.

39. For excellent overviews of Mary as "Mother of God" in early Christianity, see Reynolds, *Gateway to Heaven*, 9–49; Richard Price, "Theotokos: The Title and Its Significance in Doctrine and Devotion," in *Mary: The Complete Resource* (ed. Sarah Jane Boss; Oxford and New York: Oxford University Press, 2007), 56–73.

40. Price, "Theotokos," 56. According to the fifth-century church historian Sozomen, the term actually goes all the way back to the time of Origen in the late second to early third century A.D. (Sozomen, *Ecclesiastical History*, 7.32).

41. Translation in Gambero, *Mary and the Fathers of the Church*, 102. See also Schaff, *NPNF2*, 4:409.

42. See David M. Gwynn, *Athanasius of Alexandria: Bishop, Theologian, Ascetic, Father* (Christian Theology in Context; Oxford: Oxford University Press, 2012), 152–57; Lee Martin McDonald, *The Biblical Canon: Its Origin, Transmission, and Authority* (Grand Rapids: Baker Academic, 2007), 279–81.

43. Translation in Gambero, *Mary and the Fathers of the Church*, 162.

44. See Norman P. Tanner, S.J., *Decrees of the Ecumenical Councils* (2 vols.; London: Sheed & Ward; Washington, DC: Georgetown University Press, 1990), 44.

45. For an Eastern Orthodox view on Mary as "Mother of God," see Cunningham, *Gateway of Life*, 111–30; McGuckin, *The Orthodox Church*, 214. See also McKnight, *The Real Mary*, 125: "We Protestants can, and rightfully should, stand with the whole Church on the importance of what the Council of Ephesus decided. If 'Mother of God' means 'God-bearer' as the one who gave birth to the human Jesus who, as a single person was the God-man, then we can also stand together with Roman Catholics in affirming Mary as 'the Mother of God.'"

46. E.g., Levine, "Luke," 111; Rowe, *Early Narrative Christology*, 45.

47. See *Catechism of the Catholic Church*, no. 495. See also McKnight, *The Real Mary*, 124: "Still, we [Protestants] have to admit there is some

biblical support for calling Mary "mother of God" or "mother of the Lord."

48. See Price, "Theotokos," 56, n. 3: "The favoured Latin translation was *Dei Genetrix*, from which the standard English rendering 'Mother of God' comes. This disguises the fact that 'Mother of God' (*mētēr theou*) was a term that became widely used only much later." See D. F. Wright, "From 'God-Bearer' to 'Mother of God' in the Later Fathers," in *The Church and Mary* (ed. Robert N. Swanson; Studies in Church History 39; Woodbridge, UK: Boydell Press, 2004), 22–30.

49. See Athanasius, *Against the Arians*, 3.29.

50. For overviews of the history of Marian veneration and intercession, see esp. Reynolds, *Gateway to Heaven*, 152–245; Stephen J. Shoemaker, "Marian Liturgies and Devotion in Early Christianity," in *Mary: The Complete Resource* (ed. Sarah Jane Boss; Oxford and New York: Oxford University Press, 2007), 130–145. For a full recent study, see Stephen J. Shoemaker, *Mary in Early Christian Faith and Devotion* (New Haven: Yale University Press, 2016).

51. Quoted in Shoemaker, "Marian Liturgies and Devotion in Early Christianity," 130.

52. Translation in Gambero, *Mary and the Fathers of the Church*, 166–67.

53. Schaff, *NPNF2*, 2:379.

54. Schaff, *NPNF2*, 9b:86.

55. Translation in Daley, *On the Dormition of Mary*, 183–84.

56. Pope Pius XII even wrote an entire encyclical letter dedicated to "the Queenship of Mary," (*Ad Caeli Reginam*, October 11, 1954), which is filled with ancient quotations and well worth reading.

57. See Shoemaker, "Marian Liturgies and Devotion in Early Christianity," 132–34.

58. For arguments in favor of the historicity of the Collyridians, see Shoemaker, "Marian Liturgies and Devotion in Early Christianity," 132, 137. I would add that Ambrose of Milan also insists that "no one" give the adoration due to the Holy Spirit "to the Virgin Mary," for "Mary was the temple of God, not the God of the temple" (Ambrose, *On the Holy Spirit*, 3.11.80). The most plausible explanation for both Epiphanius and Ambrose denouncing the worship of Mary is that some people in the fourth century were actually doing it. See Schaff, *NPNF2*, 10:146.

59. Gambero, *Mary and the Fathers of the Church*, 122.

60. Translation in Williams, *The Panarion of Epiphanius*, 643–45.

61. Here the *Catechism of the Catholic Church* is quoting from Vatican II, Dogmatic Constitution on the Church, *Lumen Gentium*, no. 66.

62. See, e.g., James F. White, *Protestant Worship: Traditions in Transition*

(Louisville: Westminster John Knox, 1989); Geoffrey Wainwright, *Doxology: The Praise of God in Worship, Doctrine, and Life* (New York: Oxford University Press, 1980).

63. It is important to stress that when the Catholic Church refers to the Eucharist as a sacrifice, it does *not* mean that Christ is being "resacrificed." Instead, the *one sacrifice* of Calvary is made present. In the words of the *Catechism of the Catholic Church*: "When the Church celebrates the Eucharist, she commemorates Christ's Passover, and it is made present: *the sacrifice Christ offered once for all on the cross remains ever present*" (CCC 1364). On the sacrificial character of Jesus' actions at the Last Supper, see Brant Pitre, *Jesus and the Last Supper* (Grand Rapids: Eerdmans, 2015), 90–147, 403–43. For an Eastern Orthodox perspective, see McGuckin, *The Orthodox Church*, 288–95.

64. In the words of John Paul II: "There is an *infinite distance* between Marian veneration and worship of the Trinity and the incarnate Word." For further discussion of the difference between veneration and worship, see John Paul II, *Theotókos*, 244–54 (here 248–49); Paul VI, Apostolic Exhortation for the Right Ordering and Development of Devotion to the Blessed Virgin Mary (*Marialis Cultus*, Feburary 2, 1974), available at www.vatican.va. Regarding Eastern Orthodox veneration of Mary, see McGuckin, *The Orthodox Church*, 210–11.

Chapter 5: The Perpetual Virgin

1. See Carol E. Olson and Sandra Miesel, *The Da Vinci Hoax: Exposing the Errors in the Da Vinci Code* (San Francisco: Ignatius, 2004).

2. See Dale C. Allison, Jr., *Jesus of Nazareth: Millenarian Prophet* (Minneapolis: Fortress, 1998), 175.

3. RSVCE, slightly adapted. (As I will explain later in the chapter, I have translated Luke 1:34 literally as "since I do not know man.")

4. See Bovon, *Luke*, 42–53; Bock, *Luke*, 1:118–21; Brown, *The Birth of the Messiah*, 303–9; Fitzmyer, *The Gospel according to Luke*, 1:334–55. For a full study of the history of the interpretation of Mary's response to Gabriel, see Geoffrey Graystone, S.M., *Virgin of All Virgins: The Interpretation of Luke 1:34* (Rome: Pontifical Biblical Institute, 1968).

5. See McKnight, *The Real Mary*, 9; Fitzmyer, *The Gospel according to Luke*, 1:343–44, regarding the time between the "betrothal" (Hebrew *'erusin*) and the "taking" (Hebrew *nissu'in*) of the bride into the man's home (cf. Malachi 2:14; Matthew 1:18; 25:1–13; Mishnah, *Ketuboth* 4:4–5).

6. See Graystone, *Virgin of All Virgins*, 37–40. That is why the angel refers to Mary as Joseph's "wife" (Matthew 1:20, 24) even before he takes her into his home.

7. Gerd Lüdemann, *Virgin Birth? The Real Story of Mary and Her Son Jesus* (trans. John Bowden; Harrisburg, PA: Trinity Press International, 1998), 102.

8. Bultmann, *History of the Synoptic Tradition* (Rev. ed.; trans. John Marsh; Oxford: Basil Blackwell, 1963), 295, 296. See also John T. Carroll, *Luke: A Commentary* (New Testament Library; Louisville: Westminster John Knox, 2012), 41–42: "The question has seemed absurd to some commentators since a woman about to be married would surely expect soon to become pregnant."

9. See Fitzmyer, *The Gospel according to Luke*, 1:348; Graystone, *Virgin of All Virgins*, 114–39.

10. For this analogy, see Graystone, *Virgin of All Virgins*, 136–37.

11. J. Gresham Machen, *The Virgin Birth of Christ* (New York: Harper & Row, 1930), 143 (emphasis added). It should be noted that Machen goes on to posit the unconvincing theory of a mistranslation by Luke of an (imaginary) Semitic original.

12. See, e.g., Brown, *The Birth of the Messiah*, 304; Fitzmyer, *The Gospel according to Luke*, 1:349; Machen, *The Virgin Birth of Christ*, 144.

13. See, e.g., Brown et al., *Mary in the New Testament*, 115. Unfortunately, the claim that Mary's response is a "literary device" does not even work at the textual level. As Protestant commentators rightly point out: "The question cannot simply be a literary device to introduce 1:35 because Luke could have just continued the announcement after 1:33 with the data 1:35. In other words, 1:34 need not be supplied to get to the assertions of 1:35." Bock, *Luke*, 1:120, following I.H. Marshall, *The Gospel of Luke* (New International Greek Testament Commentary; Grand Rapids: Eerdmans, 1978), 70.

14. See Jacob Milgrom, *Numbers* (The JPS Torah Commentary; Philadelphia: Jewish Publication Society, 1990), 246: "Literally, 'you shall afflict yourselves,' chiefly by fasting, as testified by Isaiah 58:3, 5, 10. But other acts of self-denial are also implied and are understood by the rabbis as follows: 'Afflict yourselves from food and drink, bathing, anointing, [wearing] sandals, and sexual intercourse.' [Targ. Jon. Mishnah, *Yoma* 8:1] Indeed that the psalmist must specify . . . 'I afflicted myself with a fast' (Ps. 35:13), means that there are other forms of self-affliction." So too Baruch Levine, *Numbers 21–36* (Anchor Bible 4A; New York: Doubleday, 2000), 433.

15. See Milgrom, *Numbers*, 246. Mishnah, *Yoma* 8:1, clearly states that one of the categories of "self-affliction" commanded in Leviticus 16 is abstinence from sexual intercourse: "On the Day of Atonement, eating, drinking, washing, anointing, putting on sandals, and marital intercourse are forbidden." See Herbert Danby, *The Mishnah* (Oxford: Oxford University Press, 1933), 171.

16. See Ross Shepard Kraemer, ed., *Women's Religions in the Greco-Roman World* (Oxford: Oxford University Press, 2004), 28–32; Lawrence M. Wills, "Asceticism," in *The Eerdmans Dictionary of Early Judaism* (eds. John J. Collins and Daniel C. Harlow; Grand Rapids: Eerdmans, 2010), 390–92.

17. See Levine, *Numbers*, 2:440–41: "Later Jewish tradition, focused in the tractate *Nedārîm* of the Talmudim, devotes considerable attention to vows and their legal binding power ... There was special emphasis on vows of self-affliction, a subject dealt with in Numbers 30:14, especially those pronounced by women ... Such vows, if they became too extreme, led to inevitable divorce. This would be true, for instance, of a man who vowed not to have sexual relations with his wife in violation of Exodus 21:10–11, or a woman who rebelled against her husband in this regard."

18. Author's translation.

19. See Davies and Allison, *Matthew*, 1:219: "This retrospective observation *does not necessarily imply that there were marital relations later on*, for *heōs* following a negative need not contain the idea of a limit which terminates the preceding action or state (cf. Gen 49.10 LXX; Mt 10.23; Mk 9.1)." So too Brown, *The Birth of the Messiah*, 132: "As for the marital situation after the birth of the child, in itself this verse [Matt 1:25] gives us no information whatsoever."

20. Luz, *Matthew*, 1:98–99.

21. This point becomes even stronger when we realize that the Greek verb "to know" in Matthew 1:25 is in the imperfect tense, not the aorist. It could be translated (roughly) into English as "Joseph *was not knowing* her until she bore a son" (author's translation). By using the imperfect tense, Matthew puts stress on the duration of the period of abstinence, without reference to what happened afterward. See McHugh, *The Mother of Jesus in the New Testament*, 204.

22. Shortly after writing this paragraph, I happened upon the following remarkable quote from the sixth century A.D. writer, Jacob of Serug: "[Joseph] loved [Mary], he admired her, he adored her, he treasured her, he respected her, he served her, *he gazed on her as the cloud on Mount Sion, because the power of divinity dwelled within her.* Pure was his heart and holy were his thoughts too ... Pure was the Virgin and upright her spouse, of one mind." (Jacob of Serug, *Homily on the Annunciation*, 345–53). Translation in Reynolds, *Gateway to Heaven*, 98.

23. There is no need to devote any space to the argument that Mary must have had other children because Luke calls Jesus her "first-born son" (Luke 2:7). As any Jew familiar with the Scriptures would know, the term "first-born" is a technical term for *any* firstborn son of human or animal: "The LORD said to Moses, 'Consecrate to me all *the first-born*; whatever is the first to open the women among the people of Israel,

both of man and beast, is mine'" (Exodus 13:2; cf. 34:19–20). It should go without saying that this law applies to every firstborn, whether or not the human or animal ever has any other offspring. See McHugh, *The Mother of Jesus in the New Testament*, 203–4. Although the Protestant scholar François Bovon flatly denies the perpetual virginity of Mary, he admits: "As such, the adjective *prōtotokos* ["firstborn"] could not furnish a decisive argument for the existence of brothers of Jesus according to the flesh. . . ." Bovon, *Luke*, 1:85–86.

24. See Matthew 12:46–50, 13:55–56; Mark 3:31–35, 6:3; Luke 8:19–21; John 2:12, 7:3–10; Acts 1:14; cf. 1 Corinthians 9:5; Galatians 1:19.

25. For discussion of the "brothers" of Jesus, see Luz, *Matthew*, 1:98, 2:302–4; John P. Meier, *A Marginal Jew: Rethinking the Historical Jesus* (5 vols.; Anchor Yale Bible Reference Library; New Haven: Yale University Press, 1991, 1994, 2001, 2005, 2007), 1:316–32; Richard Bauckham, *Jude and the Relatives of Jesus in the Early Church* (London: T. & T. Clark, 1990), 5–133; Davies and Allison, *Matthew*, 1:219; 2:457–58; McHugh, *The Mother of Jesus in the New Testament*, 200–254.

26. See Danker, *A Greek-English Lexicon of the New Testament*, 18.

27. See Yarbro Collins, *Mark*, 774: "The second Mary should not be identified with the mother of Jesus"; Joel Marcus, *Mark* (2 vols.; Anchor Yale Bible; New Haven: Yale University Press, 2000, 2009), 2.1060; Bauckham, *Jude and the Relatives of Jesus in the Early Church*, 13: "We may first of all rule out the possibility that she is the mother of Jesus, since it is incredible that Mark, Matthew, or pre-Markan tradition should choose this way of referring to the mother of Jesus."

28. McHugh, *The Mother of Jesus in the New Testament*, 241: "Unless there is proof to the contrary, this pair of brothers must be identical with the James and Joseph mentioned earlier in the same gospels (Mt 13:55; Mk 6:3)."

29. W. D. Davies and Dale C. Allison Jr., *A Critical and Exegetical Commentary on the Gospel according to Saint Matthew* (3 vols.; International Critical Commentary; Edinburgh: T. & T. Clark, 1988, 1991, 1997), 2:458.

30. E.g., Bauckham, *Jude and the Relatives of Jesus in the Early Church*, 25–44.

31. Bauckham, *Jude and the Relatives of Jesus in the Early Church*, 15. Unfortunately, Bauckham dismisses this point, even though it is the Achilles' heel of the theory that Joseph was a widower: the Gospels make very clear that Mary, the mother of James and Joseph—the so-called brothers of Jesus—is still alive. In response to this point, Bauckham makes the unconvincing argument that there are two *different* sets of brothers: the first "James and Joseph," who are children of Joseph by a previous marriage (Mark 6:1–3; Matthew 13:55); and another "James and Joseph," who were the sons of "a Mary" who were "equally well known figures," but of whom (mysteriously) we have no other information (Bauckham, Ibid., 12–15). Needless to say, this hypothesis

strains credulity. See McHugh, *The Mother of Jesus in the New Testament*, 214 n. 13.

32. For full documentation, see Josef Blinzler, *Die Brüder und Schwestern Jesu* (Stuttgart: Verlag Katholisches Bibelwerk, 1967), 39–48.

33. Author's translation. Cf. Albert Pietersma and Benjamin G. Wright, eds., *A New English Translation of the Septuagint* (Oxford: Oxford University Press, 2007), 27, who translate *adelphoi* as "kinsfolk."

34. Josephus, *The Jewish War, Books V–VII* (trans. H. St. J. Thackeray; Loeb Classical Library 210; Cambridge: Harvard University Press, 1928), 281.

35. Unfortunately, Meier, *A Marginal Jew*, 1:327, ignores the evidence that Josephus uses "brothers" (Greek *adelphoi*) as a synonym for "relatives" (Greek *syngeneis*).

36. Compare McKnight, *The Real Mary*, 110–11, who claims that "There is nothing in any of the contexts when Jesus' brothers and sisters are mentioned to suggest that the words mean anything other than blood-brother or blood-sister." To the contrary, Joseph Fitzmyer rightly points out: "In view of the problem created by Mark 6:3 and 15:40, 47; 16:1, where 'Mary, the mother of James the Little and Joses' can scarcely be used by the evangelist to designate the mother of the person crucified on Calvary, *adelphos*, used of James, is best understood as 'kinsman, relative.'" See Joseph A. Fitzmyer, "Galatians," in *The New Jerome Biblical Commentary* (eds. R. E. Brown, J. A. Fitzmyer, and R. E. Murphy; Upper Saddle River, NJ: Prentice Hall, 1990), 783.

37. RSV, slightly adapted.

38. McHugh, *The Mother of Jesus in the New Testament*, 214: "Why does Mark not write 'in his own country and *among his brothers* and in his house'? . . . The choice of 'kinsmen' in v. 4, coming straight after v. 3, might be an indication that the brothers just mentioned could also be designated as 'kinsmen', *i.e.*, not full blood-brothers."

39. Some scholars have suggested that the text can be read as referring to four women, not three. But this is not convincing. No major English translation renders it as four women (see NRSV, NAB, ESV, RSV, etc.). The reason for this is that the natural reading of the Greek text is three women: the mother of Jesus, her sister Mary, and Mary Magdalene. See Bauckham, *Jude and the Relatives of Jesus*, 16, who rightly notes both "the extreme improbability of two sisters' having the same name Mary" and the fact that "'sister' could designate a more distant relationship such as a sister-in-law."

40. Contra Richard Bauckham, "The Brothers and Sisters of Jesus: An Epiphanian Response to John P. Meier," *Catholic Biblical Quarterly* 56 (1994): 686–700.

41. See Adele Reinhartz, "John," in *The Jewish Annotated New Testament* (2nd ed.; eds. Amy-Jill Levine and Marc Zvi Brettler; Oxford: Oxford

University Press, 2017), 215, n. on John 19:25. See also Brown, *The Gospel according to John*, 2:906: "Is 'Mary of Clopas' mentioned by John, the same as the Mary (mother of James and Joses/Joseph) . . . ? . . . If the two Marys are the same, then perhaps two of the 'brothers' of the Lord were the sons of Clopas . . . Hegesippus (ca. A.D. 150) says that Clopas was the brother of Joseph, the putative father of Jesus (Eusebius *Hist.* III ii and 32:1–5 . . .); this would make the two 'brothers' cousins of Jesus' on his father's side of the family . . . Some scholars would identify Jesus' 'mother's sister,' mentioned by John, with . . . 'Mary the mother of James and Joses/Joseph,' for then it would be clear in what way James and Joses/Joseph were 'brothers' of Jesus, namely, that they were cousins on his mother's side of the family."

42. See Marcus, *Mark*, 1:452, citing Exodus 20:12, 21:17; Leviticus 20:9.

43. On Hegesippus, see Jerome, *Lives of Illustrious Men*, 22.

44. Eusebius, *Ecclesiastical History* (2 vols.; trans. Kirsopp Lake; Loeb Classical Library 153, 265; Cambridge: Harvard University Press, 1926, 1932), 1:375. For the sake of consistency, I have rendered the Hellenized form "Symeon" (*Symeōn*) as "Simon."

45. Schaff, *NPNF2*, 1:146.

46. For example, the evidence from Hegesippus that James and Simon are Jesus' "cousins" is ignored by McKnight, *The Real Mary*, 82, 89, 110–11; Perry, *Mary for Evangelicals*; Gaventa, *Mary: Glimpses of the Mother of Jesus*.

47. Cf. Meier, *A Marginal Jew*, 1:324, who suggests that the idea that the "brothers" of Jesus were actually his "cousins" was "made up" in the fourth century by Jerome in order to defend the doctrine of Mary's perpetual virginity. It is unfortunate that Meier ignores the fact that Hegesippus identifies James and Simon as Jesus' cousins in the second century A.D. As the Anglican scholar J. H. Bernard points out: "It is difficult to understand how the doctrine of the [perpetual] Virginity of Mary could have grown up early in the second century if her four acknowledged sons were prominent Christians, and one of them bishop of Jerusalem." See J. H. Bernard, *The Gospel according to St. John* (2 vols.; International Critical Commentary; London: T. & T. Clark, 1928), 1:85.

48. Here I am following Blinzler, *Die Brüder und Schwestern Jesus*, whose arguments (to my knowledge) have never been refuted. It should be noted that my solution does not require that "Clopas" and "Alphaeus" were the same person (cf. Jerome, *Against Helvidius*, 14). I should also say something more here about the view that the "brothers" of Jesus were children of Joseph from a previous marriage (i.e., that Joseph was a widower). This view, known as the "Epiphanian" theory, suffers from at least four major weaknesses: (1) It fails to adequately explain why "James and Joseph" are called the sons of *another* Mary, who is clearly *not* the wife of Joseph (Mark 6:3; 15:40, 47; 16:1; cf. Matthew 13:55;

27:56, 61); (2) It fails to reckon with the fact that when Luke refers to "Mary the mother of *James*" (Luke 24:10) without qualifying *which* "James," he must be referring to the mother of "James" the bishop of Jerusalem, as per Luke's custom (cf. Acts 12:17; 15:13; 21:18), also known as "James the Lord's brother" (Galatians 1:19). If this Mary is the mother of James the bishop of Jerusalem, then it goes without saying that James the brother of Jesus cannot be the son of Joseph. Otherwise, Joseph would be a polygamist, not a widower! Therefore, the "mother of James" in Luke 24:10 must be some *other* Mary. (3) It fails to take into account that if Joseph had sons by a previous wife, then Jesus would *not* have been Joseph's heir (cf. Matthew 1:18–25). That honor would have gone to Joseph's actual firstborn son. (4) The Epiphanian theory is based directly on the apocryphal *Protoevangelium of James*, which even in ancient times was considered by many to be historically unreliable. For other weaknesses, see esp. McHugh, *The Mother of Jesus in the New Testament*, 208–22 (esp. 214, n. 13). Unfortunately, in his otherwise excellent work, *Jude and the Relatives of Jesus*, Bauckham does not respond to McHugh's specific criticisms of the Epiphanian hypothesis. For the view that the brothers of Jesus are the sons of another Mary and thus his "close relations," see *Catechism of the Catholic Church*, no. 500.

49. See Reynolds, *Gateway to Heaven*, 91–106.

50. Translation in Gambero, *Mary and the Fathers of the Church*, 104.

51. Translation in Gambero, *Mary and the Fathers of the Church*, 177.

52. Reynolds, *Gateway to Heaven*, 97.

53. It is worth noting here that John Chrysostom also identifies Paul's reference to "James, the Lord's brother" (Galatians 1:19) as "the son of Clopas," who "was not by birth [Jesus'] brother, but only so reputed (Chrysostom, *Homilies on Galatians* 1.19). See Schaff, *NPNF1*, 13:13.

54. Translation in Gambero, *Mary and the Fathers of the Church*, 75. Note that Origen considered the "brothers" of Jesus to be children of Joseph by a previous marriage.

55. Reynolds, *Gateway to Heaven*, 93.

56. Schaff, *NPNF2*, 6:344. The fourth-century Christian writer Epiphanius likewise describes the beliefs of a heretical group in Arabia known as the "Insulters of Mary" (Greek *Antidikomarianites*). Epiphanius refers to their rejection of Mary's perpetual virginity as a "novel madness" (*Panarion* 78,6.1). See McHugh, *The Mother of Jesus in the New Testament*, 206.

57. See Tanner, *Decrees of the Ecumenical Councils*, 115–16; Schaff, *NPNF2*, 14:313.

58. For more on the meaning of Mary's perpetual virginity, see Farkasfalvy, *The Marian Mystery*, 266; John Paul II, *Theotókos*, 116–20, 123–33; McHugh, *The Mother of Jesus in the New Testament*, 343–47.

Intriguingly, McHugh observes that "The belief that Joseph and Mary had several children all too often leads (not logically, but psychologically) to the view that Jesus himself was not virginally conceived" (ibid., 207).

59. Translation by Theodosia Tomkinson in St. Ambrose, *Exposition of the Holy Gospel according to Saint Luke*, 44 (slightly adapted).

Chapter 6: The Birth of the Messiah

1. See John Goldingay, *Isaiah 56–66* (International Critical Commentary; London: T. & T. Clark, 2014), 495; Blenkinsopp, *Isaiah*, 3:305.

2. See Blenkinsopp, *Isaiah*, 3:305–6.

3. See *The Isaiah Targum* (trans. Bruce D. Chilton; Aramaic Bible 11; Collegeville: Liturgical Press, 1990), 127.

4. H. Freedman and Maurice Simon, eds., *Midrash Rabbah* (10 vols.; London: Soncino, 1983), 2:787–88.

5. Freedman and Simon, *Midrash Rabbah*, 4:187.

6. See Aune, *Revelation*, 2:662.

7. RSVCE, slightly adapted. In the Hebrew version known as the Masoretic Text (MT), this passage occurs in Micah 5:1–2.

8. Hillers, *Micah*, 66.

9. Anderson and Freedman, *Micah*, 469.

10. For a full study of the "birth pangs of the Messiah," see Brant Pitre, *Jesus, the Tribulation, and the End of the Exile* (Grand Rapids: Baker Academic, 2005), 41–130.

11. See Collins, *The Scepter and the Star*, 76; Klausner, *The Messianic Idea in Israel*, 440–50.

12. Kevin J. Cathcart and Robert P. Gordon, *The Targum on the Minor Prophets* (Aramaic Bible 14; Collegeville: Liturgical Press, 1989), 122. For the sake of clarity, I have adjusted the translation of the Aramaic as "the Messiah" rather than "the anointed One."

13. Translation in Isidore Epstein, ed., *Hebrew-English Edition of the Babylonian Talmud* (London: Soncino, 1994), slightly adapted.

14. See Tina Pippin, "Woman in Labor, Clothed with the Sun (Rev 12:1–6, 14–17)," in *Women in Scripture: A Dictionary of Named and Unnamed Women in the Hebrew Bible, the Apocryphal/Deuterocanonical Books, and the New Testament* (eds. Carol Meyers, Toni Craven, and Ross S. Kraemer; Grand Rapids: Eerdmans, 2001), 544.

15. See especially André Feuillet, *Johannine Studies* (trans. Thomas E. Crane; New York: Alba House, 1964), 257–92. See also Ignace de la Potterie, S.J., *Mary in the Mystery of the Covenant* (trans. Bertrand S. Buby,

S.M.; New York: Alba House, 1992), 283; Le Frois, *The Woman Clothed with the Sun*, 211–62.

16. Feuillet, *Johannine Studies*, 262, citing Le Frois, *The Woman Clothed with the Sun*, 143.

17. Cf. Koester, *Revelation*, 544.

18. So Feuillet, *Johannine Studies*, 359.

19. See Koester, *Revelation*, 524; Beale, *The Book of Revelation*, 632; Aune, *Revelation*, 2:662.

20. See Pietersma and Wright, *A New English Translation of the Septuagint*, 875.

21. Feuillet, *Johannine Studies*, 263 (emphasis original).

22. See Keener, *The Gospel of John*, 2:1044–46; Brown, *The Gospel according to John*, 2.731–33.

23. See Brown, *The Gospel according to John*, 1:99–100, 517–18, 2:925–26.

24. See Keener, *The Gospel of John*, 2:1045; Brown, *The Gospel according to John*, 2:733.

25. See Brown, *The Gospel according to John*, 2:925–26; Feuillet, *Johannine Studies*, 264–65.

26. See the *Catechism of the Catholic Church*, no. 499: "The deepening of faith in the virginal motherhood led the Church to confess Mary's real and perpetual virginity even in the act of giving birth (Latin *in partu*) to the Son of God made man. In fact, Christ's birth 'did not diminish his mother's virginal integrity but sanctified it'." See also Reynolds, *Gateway to Heaven*, 76–90; O'Carroll, *Theotokos*, 361–62. It should go without saying that, from a physiological point of view, it would take a miracle of some kind for a virgin to deliver a child while retaining her physical integrity.

27. St. Irenaeus of Lyons, *On the Apostolic Preaching* (trans. John Behr; Crestwood, NY: St. Vladimir's Seminary Press, 1997), 75–76.

28. Gambero, *Mary and the Fathers of the Church*, 158–59.

29. It is worth highlighting here that one of the most ancient commentaries on Revelation we possess (late 6th–early 7th century) recognizes the allusion to Isaiah's prophecy of the painless birth in Revelation 12 and interprets Mary's labor as "free of pain." See Oecumenius, *Commentary on the Apocalypse*, 12.1, in William C. Wenrich, *Revelation* (Ancient Christian Commentary on Scripture, New Testament XII; Downers Grove: IVP Academic, 2005), 176–77.

30. Schaff, *NPNF2*, 9b:85–86.

31. See John Paul II, *Theotókos*, 94–95.

32. Heinrich Denzinger, *Compendium of Creeds, Definitions, and Declarations on Matters of Faith and Morals*, 43rd ed. (ed. Peter Hünermann; San Francisco: Ignatius, 2012), 105–6 (no. 294). For a translation of the entire

Tome of Leo, see Schaff, *NPNF2*, 14:254–58. For a similar affirmation of the virginal birth, see Leo the Great, *Sermon* 22:2: "He was engendered by a new kind of birth, conceived by a Virgin, born of a Virgin, without a father's carnal concupiscence, without injuring his Mother's integrity." Translation in Gambero, *Mary and the Fathers of the Church*, 309.

33. Significantly, when Leo's letter proclaiming the miraculous conception and birth of Jesus was read aloud at the Council of Chalcedon, the bishops present cried out: "'*This is the faith of the fathers, this is the faith of the Apostles.* So we all believe, thus the orthodox believe . . . Peter has spoken thus through Leo" (Schaff, *NPNF2*, 14:259).

34. Carmel McCarthy, *Saint Ephrem's Commentary on Tatian's Diatesseron* (*Journal of Semitic Studies* Supplement 2; Oxford: Oxford University Press, 1993), 63.

35. Translation in Gambero, *Mary and the Fathers of the Church*, 158–59.

36. See Patrick W. Skehan and Alexander A. Di Lella, *The Wisdom of Ben Sira* (Anchor Bible 39; New York: Doubleday, 1987), 469.

37. See Joel C. Elowsky, *John* (2 vols.; Ancient Christian Commentary on Scripture, New Testament IVb; Downers Grove: IVP Academic, 2007), 2:334.

38. Translation in McCarthy, *Saint Ephraim's Commentary on Tatian's Diatesseron*, 327.

39. Reynolds, *Gateway to Heaven*, 79. Cf. *Hymn on the Nativity* 7 in Schaff, *NPNF2*, 13:241.

40. Translation in Reynolds, *Gateway to Heaven*, 82. Even Augustine, who was not often at a loss for words, says of Jesus' miraculous delivery: "Who could ever comprehend this? Who could tell of it?" (Augustine, *Sermon* 215.3). Translation in Reynolds, *Gateway to Heaven*, 81.

Chapter 7: The New Rachel

1. For more on Joseph, see Maren R. Niehoff, "Joseph," in *The Eerdmans Dictionary of Early Judaism* (eds. John J. Collins and Daniel C. Harlow; Grand Rapids: Eerdmans, 2010), 822–23.

2. Schaff, *NPNF2*, 13:396.

3. William A. Kurz, S.J., *Acts of the Apostles* (Grand Rapids: Baker Academic, 2013), 121. For more on the Joseph typology in the New Testament, see Gary Anderson, *Christian Doctrine and the Old Testament* (Grand Rapids: Baker Academic, 2017), 82–91; Craig S. Keener, *Acts: An Exegetical Commentary* (4 vols.; Grand Rapids: Baker Academic, 2012, 2013, 2014, 2015), 2:1362–69; Kugel, *Traditions of the Bible*, 478. See also Ambrose of Milan, *On Joseph* 3:14.

4. See Frederick M. Strickert, *Rachel Weeping: Jews, Christians, and Muslims at the Fortress Tomb* (Collegeville: Liturgical Press, 2007).

5. See Tikva Frymer-Kensky, "Rachel," in *Women in Scripture: A Dictionary of Named and Unnamed Women in the Hebrew Bible, the Apocryphal/Deuterocanonical Books, and the New Testament* (eds. Carol Meyers, Toni Craven, and Ross S. Kraemer; Grand Rapids: Eerdmans, 2001), 138–40; Astrid Billes Beck, "Rachel," in *Anchor Bible Dictionary* (ed. David Noel Freedman; 6 vols.; Anchor Bible Reference Library; New York: Doubleday, 1992), 5:605–8; Lamontte M. Luker, "Rachel's Tomb," in *Anchor Bible Dictionary* 5:608–9.

6. Beck, "Rachel," in *Anchor Bible Dictionary* (ed. David Noel Freedman; 6 vols.; Anchor Bible Reference Library; New York: Doubleday, 1992), 5:606.

7. See Lundbom, *Jeremiah*, 2:436–37; cf. 1 Samuel 10:2.

8. Frymer-Kensky, "Rachel," 140. The idea of the deceased Rachel praying for her children is even more likely if we translate the verse not as "a voice was heard in Ramah" but literally as "a voice was heard *on a height*" (Hebrew *beramah*), as some ancients did. See Lundbom, *Jeremiah*, 2:436.

9. For a helpful overview, see Strickert, *Rachel Weeping*, 17–30.

10. Josephus, *Jewish Antiquities Books 1–3* (trans. H. St. J. Thackeray; Loeb Classical Library 242; Cambridge: Harvard University Press, 1930), 165.

11. Charlesworth, *OTP*, 2:850.

12. Freedman and Simon, *Midrash Rabbah*, 2:761.

13. See Strickert, *Rachel Weeping*, 123–27.

14. Freedman and Simon, *Midrash Rabbah*, 2:43–49.

15. Freedman and Simon, *Midrash Rabbah*, 7:49 (archaic English slightly adapted).

16. Jacob Neusner, "Can People Who Believe in Different Religions Talk Together?" *Journal of Ecumenical Studies* 28 (1991): 89–100 (here 98–99).

17. Keener, *A Commentary on the Gospel of Matthew*, 111; Brown, *The Birth of the Messiah*, 205–6.

18. Keener, *A Commentary on the Gospel of Matthew*, 110–12.

19. Flusser, Pelikan, and Lang, *Mary: Images of the Mother of Jesus*, 11–12.

20. Neusner, "Can People Who Believe in Different Religions Talk Together?", 95.

21. See Beale, *The Book of Revelation*, 625; G. K. Beale and Sean McDonough, "Revelation," in *Commentary on the New Testament Use of the Old Testament* (eds. G. K. Beale and D. A. Carson, 2007), 1122; Aune, *Revelation*, 2:680.

22. Brown et al., *Mary in the New Testament*, 230.

23. Koester, *Revelation*, 554: "her offspring include the Christian community."

24. RSVCE, slightly adapted. (I have eliminated the parentheses in the English translation, since no such parenthetical aside exists in the Greek.)

25. McKnight, *The Real Mary*, 48–49; Fitzmyer, *The Gospel according to Luke*, 1:429: "The most common interpretation of these [Simeon's] words is that of the sword of anguish that she will experience as she sees Jesus crucified and his side pierced with a lance—her role as *mater dolorosa*." See also Nolland, *Luke*, 1:121–22.

26. See Robert Alan Culpepper, *John: The Son of Zebedee, the Life of a Legend* (Minneapolis: Fortress, 2000), 72–88.

27. Translation in Bertrand Buby, S.M., *Mary of Galilee* (3 vols.; New York: Alba House, 1994, 1995, 1996), 1:157.

28. John Paul II, *Theotókos*, 234.

29. Flusser, Pelikan, and Lang, *Mary: Images of the Mother of Jesus*, 7.

30. Quoted in Shoemaker, "Marian Liturgies and Devotion in Early Christianity," 130.

31. Austin Flannery, ed., *Vatican Council II* (Northport, NY: Costello, 1992), 418–19.

32. Neusner, "Can People Who Believe in Different Religions Talk Together?," 99 (emphasis added).

Chapter 8: At the Foot of the Cross

1. Regarding death by crucifixion, see Martin Hengel, *Crucifixion in the Ancient World and the Folly of the Message of the Cross* (trans. John Bowden; Philadelphia: Fortress, 1977), 30–31.

2. Keener, *The Gospel of John*, 2:1444: "What we know of Jewish customs suggests that they invited a dying man, including one who was crucified, to settle the legal status of women for whom he was responsible; a crucified man could make his testament even from the cross." See also McKnight, *The Real Mary*, 91: "[Jesus] provided a 'last will and testament' for his mother."

3. Culpepper, *John*, 63 (emphasis added).

4. See Davies and Allison, *Matthew*, 1:185; cf. Mishnah, *Baba Bathra* 8:6.

5. Culpepper, *John*, 65. See also Brown, *The Gospel according to John*, 2:907, who translates the phrase as "the disciple took her *into his care*."

6. See Eusebius, *Church History* 6.14.7.

7. Rudolf Bultmann, *The Gospel of John*, (trans. G. R. Beasley-Murray; Philadelphia: Westminster, 1971), 484.

8. See Brown, *The Gospel according to John*, 2:924: "There is little doubt that in Johannine thought the Beloved Disciple can symbolize the Christian."

9. Edwyn Clement Hoskyns, *The Fourth Gospel* (London: Faber & Faber, 1947), 530.

10. Culpepper, *John*, 65.

11. Origen, *Commentary on the Gospel according to John* (2 vols.; trans. Ronald E. Heine; Fathers of the Church 80, 89; Washington, DC: Catholic University of America Press, 1989, 1993), 1:38.

Appendix

1. This appendix is substantially taken from Brant Pitre, *Jesus the Bridegroom: The Greatest Love Story Ever Told* (New York: Image, 2014), 169–71.